I0114609

Dr. Patrick Vance
& William Kirkpatrick Vance

Their History and Descendants

by

Delia Vance Wilson Lunsford

Copyright 2018 Delia Wilson Lunsford

Table of Contents

Preface

There are take aways I have from this project. One, we did not reproduce enough and we die too young (Heart disease? Infertility?). Two, it's an incredibly southern story with most remaining in Tennessee and Georgia. The ones that left went to Alabama, Louisiana, Virginia and Texas. I was really surprised at how little movement there was.

TECHNICAL NOTES: As a genealogist, I'm fully aware of the standards and how to quote sources; however, in order to get this finished in a timely manner I have opted to forgo some of those proofs. Indeed, in numerous cases, did not search for the proofs. My guilt has to be borne in order to get this done!

So just because a date is entered or just because the records that come after the first few generations are here does not mean this is the fully correct record of this family. I have had some relatives vet the data in their bits of family and in general I was careful about what I did accept. Mistakes cannot be avoided though.

I am producing a digital version for corrections. The print book shall stand as originally written unless I have requests and financial assistance to produce another version for print. The books are print on demand so the cost would be minimal. The digital version also has hyperlinks in the table of contents and in the text as well. The digital version is only available via my website at cvillegenie. com/shop. Purchasing both on my website will reduce pricing for the digital version and updated digital versions are always available for download.

My main purpose was to get as much information together about Dr. Patrick and his sons before I moved from Virginia. The footnotes included are mainly from that research. Hopefully, there's enough here so that a future researcher can pick up where I left off in order to add new tales of the Vances in Lexington. It was fascinating to dig into records there and get to know the area. I'm still in wonder at the vistas - to think that the settlers drove down beside those mountains along the same paths one can drive on today. They must have thought they had arrived in heaven!

I have used a genealogical method to enumerate the families. It is one that I feel is simply not easy to follow but it is what the software has to do in order to speed up this process. Each person who has children is listed with a number; each person who is part of a family is listed with a roman numeral. If with both, then there are children. Just follow the links listed in each case: the (page xx) is a hyperlink in the digital version. All are listed as generations. Though there is no generation 8 listed, there are children of that generation but there is only one that I actually know of, my first cousin's grandchild born December 2016.

You may contact me via the forms on cvillegenie.com or wiztech4zc.com.

Delia Vance Wilson Lunsford
April, 2018

Dr. Patrick Vance of Lexington, Virginia

The most striking story about Dr. Patrick Vance of Lexington, Rockbridge County, Virginia, is about scalped heads. It is a tiny bit of the story of this Tennessee Vance family but it is simply the best known piece. The earliest known mention of Dr. Patrick is actually in the Draper Manuscripts[1]:

> *Surgery and surgical instruments were of the most primitive kind on the early frontier. During the Christian campaign, while the men were quartered at Long Island, a Dr. Vance discovered a treatment for scalped persons. He bored holes in the skull in order to create a new flesh covering for the exposed bone. On being called away he taught James Robertson how to perform the operation. Frederick Calvit, a scalped patient, was brought in and Robertson had a chance to practice upon him — "he [Vance] bored a few holes himself, to show the manner of doing it." He further declares: 'I have found that a flat pointed, straight awl is the best instrument to bore with as the skull is thick and somewhat difficult to penetrate. When the awl is nearly through the instrument should be borne more lightly upon. The time to quit boring is when a reddish fluid appears on the point of the awl. I bore at first about one inch apart and as the flesh appears to rise in these holes I bore a number more between the first, etc.* * * *The scalped head cures slowly. It skins remarkably slow, generally taking two years."*

More information on that first appearance in Virginia is available in a history of Sullivan County, Tennessee: "Patrick Vance appointed third surgeon with pay of assistant" The footnote numbered two is the description above. That appointment line is from the orderly book of Camp Lady Ambler, Oct. 20, 1776, and is a detailed description of the Christian Campaign against the Cherokees that lasted until December of that year.[2]

Another account in James Robertson's own words, from The Philadelphia Medical and Physical Journal, Volume 2, 1805, p. 27[3] reads:

> *"III. Remarks on the Management of the Scalped-Head. By Mr. James Robertson, of Nashville, in the State of Tenessee. Communicated to the Editor, by Felix Robertson, M. D., of the same place. In the year 1777, there was a Doctor Vance, about the Long-Islands of Holsten, who was there attending on the different garrisons, which were embodied on the then frontiers of Holsten, to guard the inhabitants against the depradations of the Cheerake-Indians. This Doctor Vance came from Augusta-County, in Virginia. In March of the same year, Frederick Calvit was badly wounded, and nearly the whole of his head skinned."*

1. https://en.wikipedia.org/wiki/Lyman_Draper
2. Taylor, Oliver, Historic Sullivan, a History of Sullivan County, Tennessee, with brief Biographies of the Makers of History (Bristol, Tennessee: The King Printing Company, 1909), 65-66.
3. https://books.google.com/books?id=GCgdAQAAMAAJ

So according to both accounts, Dr. Patrick was on Long Island in the Holsten River which flows from Virginia into Tennessee. Long Island is at Kingsport and according to Wikipedia:

> "The Long Island of the Holston River was an important site for the Cherokee, colonial pioneers, and early settlers of the region. The site was used as a staging ground for people following the Wilderness Road into Kentucky. It was a sacred council and treaty site among the Cherokee people. The Timberlake Expedition of 1761–1762 used it as its point of origin and return. It was from here that Daniel Boone, in 1775, began to clear the Wilderness Road, which extended through the Cumberland Gap into Kentucky."[4]

Who Was Patrick Vance & Where Did He Come From?

I can theorize that he came out of Pennsylvania as most of the Shenandoah Valley Scotch-Irish came down the Great Wagon Trail[5], now known as US 11 or Lee Highway in Virginia. During my visit to Lexington, this was stressed to me several times. The settlers had come from the north, not from the east.

We do not know when he was born in Ireland nor his actual death date but his family origins are known by virtue of a book entitled An Account Historical and Genealogical, from the Earliest Days till the Present Time of the Family of Vance in Ireland, Vans in Scotland, Anciently Vaux in Scotland. and England of DeVaux in France (Latin De Vallibus.)[6]:

> "George of Raneel, parish of Inver, Donegal, was, we doubt not, grandson to Rev, John Vance, and one of the ten sons of Patrick Vans. He was succeeded in Raneel, by his second son, Thomas, whose son. Hugh Vance, of Gortward, Doran, also in Inver, had two sons, first, _Patrick, who emigrated to America unmarried_; second, Hugh, an officer of excise, and four daughters, married respectively to Messrs. McKee, McGonigal, O'Donnell, and Carscadden, and had families." (p. 52)

A Vance researcher was able to access a version of Balbirnie's book that had handwritten notes in addition to the above passage:

> "The copy of the 1860 version that I have is a copy of the one that Balbirnie gave to the parents of his 2nd wife and inscribed in his own handwriting "To Mr and _Mrs Joseph McElwaine, Ballyronan, County Derry, With the kind regards of their_

4. Long Island (Tennessee), https://en.wikipedia.org/wiki/Long_Island_(Tennessee), accessed 8 Oct 2017.

5. https://en.wikipedia.org/wiki/Great_Wagon_Road#Great_Wagon_Road:_Philadelphia_to_Roanoke.2C_Virginia_.28circa_1754.29_.E2.80.93_approximately_395_miles_.28636.C2.A0km.29

6. Balbirnie, William, an Account Historical and Genealogical, from the Earliest Days till the Present Time of the Family of Vance in Ireland, Vans in Scotland, Anciently Vaux in Scotland and England of DeVaux in France (Latin De Vallibus.), (Cork, Ireland: JM Noblett, 1860).

affectionate Son-in-law The Author, Cork, 16 January 1862." In this book he had placed an astrick just above (Dr) Patrick's name and made notes so small they are difficult to read and quote exactly – but in the back of that book he adds great detail about this family. WHY? Not only to correct the error about emigrating unmarried but because at this point in time (those notes written in the 1870's, after 1871) he was a "part" of this family. Dr. Patrick's grandson, Dr. Wm Nicholas and William Balbirnie both married sisters after the death of their first wives. These sisters were Balbirnie's second cousins. Helen McElwaine married Dr. Wm Nicholas Vance and Margarite McElwaine married Wm Balbirnie. Both named a daughter Charlotte.

Therefore Balbirnie was privy to much information on that family and he wrote:

"At page 52 of this account is it stated that Hugh Vance of Gortward Co. Donegal – his eldest who emigrated to America unmarried. This last assertion we have discovered to be erroneous. Patrick was a student of Medicine, studied at Edinburgh and graduated as a physician at that university. Previously to emigrating he married a Scotch lady a Miss Graham by whom he had 3 sons, 1st Hugh, evidently was named after his paternal grandfather. 2nd David Graham probably after his maternal grandfather and 3rd Wm. Kirkpatrick Vance." (Vance Family Association Newsletter, July 1987, p. 56)

That newsletter also contains the photostat copy of the page with Balbirnie's notations and you can see the addition of Wm Kirkpatrick's and Wm Nicholas' names into the family tree portion.

I believe the author is Mary Virginia Reed who we all owe a great debt to. Without her work (and the work of many others) we would not have as complete a picture of Dr. Patrick's family.

Of note, is that Dr. Patrick's line included quite a few generations of Irish born - at least six. Not your usual Scotch-Irish at all as the family were landed and at some point also royalty. Jamie Vans, Laird of Barnbarrouch, Scotland, has written a short piece, *Origin of the Irish Vances*, which is not available online or purchasable in print in which he debunks the existence of the famed Lancelot Vance of Londonderry and gives us more information on the proven details of the Irish Vances.[7]

The linage seems certain but not with accurate birth dates. Jamie's line is fully established and he coordinates the research and is the contributor to the Vance DNA project that has proven the DNA connections between Dr. Patrick's line and the Vans/Vances of Scot-

---

7. Vans, Jamie, P A Vans, Origin of the Irish Vances, a review of the evidence (Vans Family Archive, 1983, 2001, 2007)

land.[8]

In the appendix, I have included the full ancestor report – which begins with Robert, King of Scotland separately up to Dr. Patrick. It is an agreed upon lineage but by no way accurate with dates.

Medical Degree

The University of Edinburgh has on line the names of students back to 1587 but Patrick Vance's name is not in the database. They state, however, not all students' names are in the database.[9] They also have the images of Laureation & Degrees which are signed by the graduates. I did not find his name there either. I do not recall how many years I looked at the time but I would expect it to be unlikely that his name would appear there and not be in the online database but transcription errors are certainly possible. For anyone who wishes to sift through these records they are online here: http://archives.lib.ed.ac.uk/alumni/ld.php

If he were already in America by the fall of 1776 and had medical training, I would speculate that he was over 20 and therefore born before 1755. Two things one must keep in mind is first that medical training was not as long as it is today and two, he could have started quite early in that training. Jamie Vans states that there is evidence in the lineage of men starting very early.

> Sir Patrick Vaus himself, grandfather (or just possibly even father) of the Rev. John of Kilmacrenan, appears to have been no more than 15 years old when appointed Rector of Wigtown in 1545.[10]

Though that is much earlier than our Patrick, it still might establish a pattern in the family. When the first medical school was established in 1765 at the University of Pennsylvania, however, the minimum age for a medical degree was 24 and the awarding of a bachelor's degree previously.[11] Starting that education was more loose: "The concept of getting accepted to medical school did not exist. One paid the fees and matriculated."[12]

---

8. http://www.vancegenealogy.com/
9. http://collections.ed.ac.uk/alumni/rosner
10. Vans, Jamie, 13
11. http://www.archives.upenn.edu/histy/features/1700s/medsch.html
12. http://www.archives.upenn.edu/histy/features/medical_lecture_tickets/narrative.html

The Homestead

By the time Patrick purchased 150 plus 70 acres of land in the forks of the James River and Whistle Creek on 5 May 1778,[13] he had at least one if not two children for David may have been born in 1778. He also served on the first grand jury that year on the second of May.[14]

He then sold part of the homestead in 1787. (Book B, 617) No one has been able to find more deeds but the indexes at the courthouse are incomplete - the first sale is not in the index. The picture above is from a book that called it the Thomas J Wilson house in 1936.[15] That book states it is located four miles north of Natural Bridge, placing it about 6 to 8 miles south of Lexington. Yet, the only Whistle Creek known today is north of Lexington. The river that flows through Lexington is the Maury which does intersect with Whistle Creek. That area is also near the Old Monmouth Cemetery where

13. Rockbridge County Deeds., Book A, 14-15.
14. Morten, Oren F, A History of Rockbridge County Virgnia (Baltimore: Regional Publishing Company, 1920) 82.
15. McClung, James W, The Historical Significance of Rockbridge County (Staunton, Va: McClure Company, Inc, 1939) 218-219.

the church that Dr. Patrick probably attended first. That is on Whistle Creek. That area was called the Forks of the James by 1740 and appears to actually reference everything between the Maury and the James rivers.[16]

I was able to determine that the Thomas J Wilson house was sited near Natural Bridge and I found a house that looks similar. That one is recorded in the Historic District records as being built in 1790 and listed as the earliest.[17] The James River is only south of Natural Bridge; the Maury meets it below the town of Glasgow at the mountains' edge. That house is definitely not near Whistle Creek. Since the house I found is so similar looking, I believe that either it was mistakenly identified as the Vance house or that the Wilson house is now gone. The author of the book that picture appears in was, according to research librarians at Washington & Lee, not liked and was known to surreptitiously take pictures of homes. His information is, therefore, suspect.

At least one of the deeds for Dr Patrick's house was witnessed by W Lyle; we have to assume this is William Lyle who became William's guardian. He was specifically Lexington based and witnesses to deeds are usually neighbors and not just friends or family. That heightens the probability of that property being located closer to Lexington. Church membership is also a factor here - it is highly unlikely that Dr. Patrick would be a member of a Lexington Church if he lived near Natural Bridge. There is a Presbyterian church not far from the area in Natural Bridge: High Bridge, founded 1770.

Presbyterian Churches - Memberships

In trying to decipher which church and in turn perhaps find a possible burial spot, one has to talk Presbyterian. It should not be too much of a surprise to Dr. Patrick's descendants but there were a glut of Presbyterian meeting houses, churches and sub-churches in the area. (I myself grew up in Georgia where the Baptists reigned supreme and us Presbyterians were the odd balls.) Lexington was a hotbed of Presbyterianism in comparison. In the Old Monmouth Cemetery a plaque explains the evolution of New Monmouth

---

16. http://www.rootsweb.ancestry.com/~varockbr/rkchurch.htm
17. https://www.nps.gov/nr/feature/places/pdfs/15001047.pdf

Church. First organized in 1746 and built in 1748, they built a new building in 1767 and the church became Hall's Meeting House. In 1789, it became New Monmouth and shortly after that birthed a sub/sister church, Lexington Presbyterian, which was located in town. The two churches shared the same pastor, William Graham, a famous figure, for the next 30 years.[18] The famous Stonewall Jackson Cemetery was started in 1789 on that property before the church building was erected.

The earliest subscribers' list is from 1786 which would be for New Monmouth.

We the subscribers do promise to pay for the Labours of the Rev'd Mr. Hogg yearly and every year for his Labours as a minister if the meeting house or place of worship Continues where it now is, the sums to our names annexed.--September 19, 1786. (Signed), Samuel Miller, Robert Lawson, Robt. McCampbell, James Cunningham, Robt. McKee, John Gilmore, Isaac Lawson, George Smith, John Wilson, Wm. McKee, John McElwee, Hugh Were, Wm. Presly, Samuel Wilson, James McMath, Joseph Caldwell, John McKee, James McKee, John Moor, James Logan, John Hamilton, Chas. Kirkpatrick, Patrick Vance, Mathew Hannah, James Moor, Henry Skeen, Robt. Cravins, John McKemy, Abraham Goodpasture, John Cooper, George Townsley.[19]

That list varies greatly from the other lists which appear to be for the Lexington church. They are dated May 6, 1788, April 20, 1789 and one undated subscriber's list that is entitled "A List of those who have p^d Rev^d Wm Graham their Sallary due before Novr 90" where Patrick had paid 18 shillings.[20] It does appear these lists are done in a chronological fashion of membership dates because the Lexington lists are all in the same order. Another undated list separates out the Lexington subscribers and Patrick is not listed with the Lexington subscribers.

Two of Dr. Patrick's fellow Presbyterians who also performed the inventory after his death were Mathew Hanna and William Alexander, both of who lived in town and are buried in the Stonewall Jackson Cemetery. They were also members of the Lexington Church - appearing on each list. This suggests a close relationship between the three men. They do appear on a list and each with their wives, William and Agnes, Mathew and Martha and Patrick and Mary.

---

18. http://www.lexpres.org/history/

19. "Papers from the Pastorates of Dr. Wm Graham and Dr. Geo A Baxter, 1776 tp 1822", Washington & Lee University Lerner Library Holdings, Lexington, VA.

20. W & Lee, 112 folder 2 Miscellaneous Papers, 1771-1798,nd

Either the Rockbridge Historical Society or the Union Theological Seminary has this list on microfilm but I was never able to find it but the text is online. Ireland is listed for both Patrick and Mary and gives death dates for most of the other members but not them.[21]

Also on some of the lists is William Lyle who paid a bond for Hugh's guardianship in late 1791.[22] Hugh, being over 14, was legally able to choose his guardian and he chose his mother, Mary. On 5 April 1796 William Kirkpatrick chose William Lyle as his guardian.[23] In those times that meant more about managing property than it did about raising a child until the age of his majority (21). This would not have been necessary if there was no real estate.[24] So Lyle may have been another close friend of the family. He lived in town until the "great fire" of 11 April 1796 when he moved to his farm, Oakley, said to be four miles north of Lexington. He was a well-to-do merchant, gentleman (meaning a man of substance who doesn't have to actually work[25]), mill owner[26] and the ranking officer (lieutenant) in Lexington during the revolution.[27]

William Kirkpatrick turned 21 in 1801 so most likely Dr. Patrick's property was not disposed of until after that when all three sons could legally make decisions. Sometimes that process could take years though and one researcher did report that there was a land sale as late as 1811. I looked at the indexes for years before and after 1811 but did not go through each deed. I never found any evidence of another property transaction but I do think there is one.

There are about 100 unmarked or broken stone graves in the Stonewall Jackson Cemetery that date from that era, leaving me to believe that is where Patrick and Mary are buried. Of course, there is still a possibility they were buried in Old Monmouth. Findagrave.com only lists 72 graves in Monmouth; at least six date before 1800 which is a low number for a church that has been in existence since 1746. So I assume many missing gravestones there as well. That

21. http://files.usgwarchives.net/va/rockbridge/churches/lexpres.txt
22. Rockbridge County Court Order Book 3 p 416.
23. Rockbridge County Court Order Book 4 p. 149.
24. http://www.genfiles.com/articles/orphans-guardians/
25. Morton, 80.
26. Morton, 552.
27. Lyle, Oscar K, Lyle Family, The Ancestry and Posterity of Matthew, John, Daniel and Samuel Lyle, Pioneer Settlers in America (Brooklyn, NY: Lecouver Press, 1912) 292-293.

cemetery is not being maintained - it is overgrown and though close to the road, not really accessible but it is quite small from a distance.

Other appearances of Patrick includes the tax/tithables lists of 1778, 1782, 1783, 1787, 1789 as well as suits against John Wallace in 1782 and 1783.[28] He also sued the estate of Samuel Wallace in 1788.[29] Along with Hugh Wier and Samuel Wilson, he witnessed a deed in 1778, James Shanks to Thomas Wilson. Thomas Wilson also served on that first grand jury with Patrick as did Hugh Wier.

One note of interest is about education. Dr. Patrick's minister, William Graham, was the first president of Liberty Hall and therefore of Washington & Lee University. The school, originally Augusta Academy, was renamed in 1776 and then moved to Lexington in 1782. It granted its first bachelor's degree in 1785 (among its first graduates was Samuel Houston of Alamo fame) and is the ninth oldest institution of higher learning in America.[30] It was a Presbyterian school, managed by the Hanover Presbytery and came in a period of "liberal education". It has been said that Presbyterians at that time came to believe that education "could solve the most difficult problems and resolve the most persistent tensions in their society."[31] Though this sets the scene for an educated household and church life for the Vance boys, their Father's early death may have prevented (due to lack of money) their attendance at Liberty Hall. These influences, coupled with Dr. Patrick's medical background, could have contributed to William Kirkpatrick's two oldest sons becoming doctors as well as his own participation in education in Greenville.

Mary was appointed administrator of Patrick's estate on 5 April 1791. The inventory of Dr. Patrick's effects is an indication of some wealth as it includes 6 silver teaspoons, tongs and a case, in addition to a mare, cow, pig, a tea table, two cupboards and chest of drawers. Dated April 16th 1791, the inventory proves his death could have possibly been in late 1790 as well, of course, as early

28. Rockbridge County Court Order Book 1, p 351-352, 355, 381.
29. Rockbridge County Court Order Book 3
30. https://en.wikipedia.org/wiki/Washington_and_Lee_University
31. Miller, G. Howard, The Revolutionary College: American Presbyterian Higher Education, 1707-1837 (New York: New York University Press, 1976).

1791.[32]

Dr. Patrick and Mary Graham did have three boys, Hugh, David and William Kirkpatrick. Hughey b.1776 d.1862 may not be buried with his wife, Sarah Law but is buried in Deck Cemetery, Washington County, Virginia, with his son, Patrick J b.1804 d.17 Jun 1876[33] and probably his daughter, Mary J b.1814 d.1835.[34] Patrick had 7 children with his wife Katherine Fleenor and at least 23 grandchildren. He was a farmer in Kinderhook, Washington County, Virginia, who died of tuberculosis.[35]

David Graham Vance was born around 1780 and died 1823. He married Theodosia whose last name may have been Harvey. (Their surviving son was named James Harvey Vance - his 1880 census lists his mother as being from New Jersey.) They had six children (5 girls and 2 boys) and at least 28 grandchildren. David owned an inn in Jonesborough, Tennessee, from an early age[36] which his wife continued after his death at about age 50. More about his military service can be found on the Findagrave.com page.[37]

William Kirkpatrick "Patrick" Vance, 1780-1852

William Kirkpatrick Vance b.2 March 1780 d.28 Nov 1852[38] married Keziah Robertson b.17 Jul 1791 d.1 Nov 1843, daughter of Charles Robertson and Susan who may have been a Harvey. (That would explain the middle name of the second born, James Harvey Vance.) Their marriage is recorded in Morton's History of Rockbridge County with no date and William referred to as Patrick.[39] This may indicate a record of that marriage in Virginia but I did not find it. She was, however, from Tennessee and the state lines varied over the years.

---

32. Rockbridge County Wills & Deeds, vol. I, 385.
33. https://www.findagrave.com/cgi-bin/fg.cgi?page=gr&GSsr=41&GS-cid=2601056&GRid=157198413&
34. https://www.findagrave.com/cgi-bin/fg.cgi?page=gr&GSsr=41&GS-cid=2601056&GRid=157198392&
35. Washington County, Virginia Deaths, 1853-1885, ancestry.com database
36. Goodspeeds History of Tennessee, http://www.newrivernotes.com/topical_books_1887_history_of_tennessee.htm
37. http://www.findagrave.com/cgi-bin/fg.cgi?page=gr&GRid=147544445
38. Gravestone, https://www.findagrave.com/cgi-bin/fg.cgi?page=gr&GRid=25241415
39. Morton, 537.

Keziah is much more important in this Vance family than most folks have realized. Besides the incredible history of her family, both the Robertsons[40] and Seviers[41], in Tennessee and American history, Keziah's grandmother was Susanna Nichols (grandfather Charles); Susanna's mother was Mary Jefferson (father Julius Nichols); Mary Jefferson was the daughter of Field Jefferson and therefore first cousin to President Thomas Jefferson. Living in Charlottesville, home to Jefferson, Monticello and Jefferson's university has made me very aware of how many folks here are related to Thomas Jefferson. Now I find that the Vances are as well!

William K's first appearance in the records that is known was in 1808 in Washington County, Tennessee where he owed the estate of Sam Wilson $10 for military instructions.[42] The Washington county seat is Jonesborough and considered to be the first Tennessee town. We know that David Graham may have been the innkeeper there as early as 1800 so it's reasonable to believe William K moved there as well once he reached his majority in 1801 or even before. It is considered to be the center of the abolitionist movement in the south, and eastern Tennessee does have an interesting history with the civil war which did figure highly into family movement later in the nineteenth century. Washington County lies beneath Sullivan County on the Tennessee - Virginia border with I81 going through the middle of it. The major town in Sullivan county is Kingsport where his son James Harvey settled later.

He did fight along side his brother, David, in the War of 1812 as a sergeant in the Williams' Mtd E Tennessee Vols.[43] Wm K first bought a lot in Greeneville in 1816 and more lots the next year so the family may have moved in 1816 to Greeneville.

"He opened a Leather Store, stocking Saddles, Bridles and Collars" of his own manufacturing and needed ten or twelve journeymen shoemakers and saddlers in Jonesborough.[44] Goodspeed's History of

40. Williams, Samuel Cole, History of the Lost State of Franklin (Johnson City, Tennessee: Over Mountain Press 1933) 306.

41. http://www.oldplaces.org/eTennessee/RobertSevier.htm

42. Vance Family Newsletter, October 1999, p 149.

43. NARA M602. Alphabetical card index to the compiled service records of volunteer soldiers who served during the War of 1812., roll M602_0214.

44. Fink, Paul M, Jonesborough : the first century of Tennessee's first town, 1776-1876 (Johnson

Jonesborough called him a saddler and he was remembered by Gen A E Jackson as saddler in 1815 in Jonesborough.[45]

He was a trustee (commissioner) for Greene County from 1820-1834 (Goodspeed) and also was a trustee for the Greeneville College. He bought an inn / tavern in 1821: it was originally called the De-Woody Tavern and Wm K renamed it the Bell Tavern. That inn site today is the General Morgan Inn as the original structure was demolished in 1886 and a hotel built there instead. At the same time, his Uncle David Graham and later David's wife, Theodosia, operated a tavern in Jonesborough with the same name. Both were advertised as "at the sign of the Bell". During the civil war, Joshua Lane operated the tavern. There was either the original or copy of an advertisement for William's inn online but it is no longer available.[46]

Two of his sons became doctors and the third, David Graham, inherited the business and worked in the inn before his father's death. The youngest son, Patrick Henry, never had children or seemed to do more than work as a saddler.

William moved to Kingsport before the census of 1850 probably after Keziah's death in 1843. In March of 1852, William put into place a retirement plan and his wishes in place of a will. He was about seven months from his death and was probably failing at the time. He sold much of his holdings to his son, David, after stating that his trustees would furnish William "a decent and comfortable support and maintenance during his natural life allowing said Wm.K. Vance to choose his own residence among his children. Said trustee shall further out of said property furnish to Harriet G. Vance a decent and comfortable support during her life or untill her marriage should such event occur." Upon his death, the remaining property was to be sold and all proceeds plus any balance of money in the hands of his trustees was to be divided among his children.[47] As David stated in the 1850 census that he was a inn keeper, he must have been working at the inn primarily and decided to take on the debt for the inn rather than sell it.

City, Tennessee, 1989: Overmountain Press) 50.
45. http://www.newrivernotes.com/topical_books_1887_history_of_tennessee.htm
46. http://www.generalmorganinn.com/wp-content/uploads/2011/03/GMI-History.pdf
47. Sullivan County Deed Book, vol 17, page 53.

William Kirkpatrick Vance and Keziah Robertson had the following children:

i. CHARLES ROBERTSON VANCE was born on 23 Apr 1809 in Washington County, Tennessee and died on 16 Apr 1825 in Tennessee.[48]

ii. (4) JAMES HARVEY VANCE MD (page 16) was born on 4 Jan 1811 in Greeneville, Tennessee. He died on 7 Jul 1893[49] in Kingsport, Tennessee. He married JANE SEVIER, daughter of Valentine "The Red Fox" Sevier and Nancy Agnes Dinwiddie Servier, on 26 Aug 1832 in Warm Springs, North Carolina. She was born on 23 Aug 1818 in Greeneville, Tennessee, and died on 1 Mar 1886 in Kingsport, Tennessee. They had nine children, but only three had children of their own.

iii. (5) DAVID GRAHAM VANCE (page 17)was born on 4 Oct 1812 in Jonesborough, Tennessee. He died on 26 Jan 1878 in Buford, Georgia. He married (1) MARY JANE MCCORKLE, daughter of John McCorkle and Mary "Polly" Cunningham, on 10 Jun 1834 in Washington County, Tennessee. She was born on 30 Jun 1816 in Tennessee. She died on 21 May 1859 in Greenville, Tennessee. He married (2) CATHARINE BRITTON, daughter of Major James Britton II and Margaret Pauline "Polly" Robinson, on 17 Nov 1859 in Greene, Tennessee. She was born in 1821 in Greene County, Tennessee. David and Mary Jane had eleven children.

iv. (6) WILLIAM NICHOLAS VANCE, MD, (page 20) was born on 12 Nov 1814 in Greeneville, Tennessee, and died on 12 Feb 1895 in Sullivan County, Tennessee. He married (1) SARAH ANNE NETHERLAND on 1 Oct 1839 in Kingsport, Tennessee. She was born on 28 Mar 1820 in Kingsport, Tennessee, and died on 13 Feb 1868 in Bristol, Tennessee (of consumption). He married (2) HELENA MCILWAINE on 15 Aug 1871 in County Cork, Ireland. She was born on 25 Dec 1850 in Ireland and died on 26 Mar 1882 in Sullivan County, Tennessee.

v. CATHERINE MARIA VANCE was born on 14 Jul 1817 in Greeneville, Tennessee, and died on 4 Jun 1832 in Greeneville.[50]

vi. PATRICK HENRY VANCE was born on 13 Oct 1819 in Greeneville, Tennessee. He married (1) NANCY C HARVEY on 9 Mar 1847 in Washington County, Tennessee. She was born in 1829 in Tennessee and died before 1860. Then he married (3) REBECCA REMINE, daughter of Hiram Remine and Nancy, on 15 Jul 1860 in Greene, Tennessee. She was born in 1841 in Virginia. Patrick Henry may have died between his marriage and 1870. He was living with his brother, David Graham in 1860 and is listed as a Master Saddler. I found a reference to him that said he died during the Civil War in Cincinnati, Ohio, but I can find no proof of that.[51] I did find one invoice for saddles during the war signed by P H Vance.[52]

vii. (7) CAROLINE FLORENCE VANCE (page 22) was born on 7 Nov 1822 in Greeneville, Tennessee, and died on 7 Dec 1881 in

48. Gravestone, http://www.findagrave.com/cgi-bin/fg.cgi?page=gr&GRid=25241417

49. Gravestone, https://www.findagrave.com/cgi-bin/fg.cgi?page=gr&GRid=88112226

50. Gravestone, https://www.findagrave.com/cgi-bin/fg.cgi?page=gr&GRid=25241419

51. Speer, William S, Sketches of Prominent Tennesseans : Containing Biographies and Records of Many of the Families who Have Attained Prominence in Tennessee (Baltimore, MD, Genealogical Publishing Co, 2010) 336.

52. https://www.fold3.com/image/55106408

Cleveland, Tennessee. She married PLEASANT M CRAIGMILES on 17 Jan 1843 in Greene County. He was born on 4 Oct 1813 in Tennessee and died on 8 Sep 1876 in Cleveland, Tennessee.

viii.   HOUSTON VANCE was born on 14 Feb 1825. He died on 11 Dec 1827 in Greene County, Tennessee.

ix.   (8) KEZIAH P "KIZZIE" VANCE (page 22) was born on 10 Dec 1825 in Washington County, Tennessee and died on 17 Nov 1902 in Knox County, Kentucky. She married OLIVER PERRY HERNDON 2 Mar 1846 in Washington County, Tennessee. He was born on 4 Apr 1826 in Cumberland Ford, Kentucky and died on 17 Jul 1897 in Barbourville, Kentucky.

x.   (9) HARRIET GRAHAM VANCE (page 23) was born on 31 May 1829 in Greene County, Tennessee. She died on 27 Nov 1926 in Dallas, Texas. She married PLEASANT LAWSON THORNTON. He was born on 5 Nov 1831 in Georgia and died on 4 Mar 1907 in Grayson County, Texas.

xi.   (10) SUSAN N VANCE (page 24) was born in 1833 in Tennessee and died on 30 Mar 1873 in Sullivan County, Tennessee. She married JAMES STROTHER PATTON in 1850. He was born on 19 Oct 1827 in Kingsport, Tennessee and died on 28 Jun 1903 in Kingsport.

Generation 3

4.   JAMES HARVEY VANCE, MD, (William Kirkpatrick[2], Dr. Patrick[1]) was born on 4 Jan 1811 in Greeneville, Tennessee and died on 7 Jul 1893 in Kingsport, Tennessee. He married JANE SEVIER, daughter of Valentine "The Red Fox" Sevier and Nancy Agnes Dinwiddie, on 26 Aug 1832 in Warm Springs, North Carolina. She was born on 23 Aug 1818 in Greeneville, Tennessee, and died on 1 Mar 1886 in Kingsport, Tennessee.

He invested in a glass factory: Williams, Vance and Company formed in 1839 with James providing money instead of active participation but it never got off the ground. Fink said "It must have been some sort of promotional scheme for nothing further has been in local newspapers or elsewhere concerning the plant or its operations."[53]

Images of his medical school thesis are online.[54] He wrote about cholera in 1832 and he also attended Tusculum College.

James Harvey Vance and Jane Sevier had the following children:

i.   (11) CHARLES ROBERTSON VANCE, lawyer, (page 24) was born on 22 Aug 1835 in Cherokee, Tennessee, and died on 12 Nov 1911 in Bristol, Tennessee. He married MARGARET JANE NEWLAND, daughter of Joseph Newland, Jr, and Rebecca Maxwell Anderson, on 16 Oct 1860 in Arcadia, Tennessee. She was born on 28 Mar 1838 in Arcadia, Tennessee, and died on 8 Apr 1914 in Bristol, Tennessee.

ii.   MARIA C VANCE was born on 29 Jan 1839 in Washington County, Tennessee. She died before 1930 in Tennessee. She married JOHN RUTLEDGE KING on 7 May 1878. He was born on 13 Apr 1817 in Roanoke County, Virginia. He died before 1900. He was a

53. Fink, 49.
54. http://kdl.kyvl.org/catalog/xt7t7659f47j_1

Presbyterian minister and had a previous marriage and children.

iii. ANNE ELIZABETH VANCE was born on 22 Aug 1841 in Washington County, Tennessee, and died on 25 Jun 1858 in Sullivan County, Tennessee.

iv. KEZIA VANCE was born on 28 Dec 1843 in Washington County, Tennessee. She died on 5 Apr 1917 in Kingsport, Tennessee.

v. (12) WILLIAM VANCE V, (page 25) lawyer, was born in 1848 in Sullivan County, Tennessee. He died before 1900 in Tennessee. He married MARY FRANCIS "FANNIE" MILLER on 15 Sep 1869 in Hawkins, Tennessee. She was born in 1848 in Tennessee.

vi. NANCY "NANNIE" VANCE was born on 9 Jan 1853 in Sullivan County, Tennessee. She died on 30 Jan 1939 in Scott County, Virginia. She married ISAAC ANDERSON NEWLAND, son of Joseph Newland, Jr, and Rebecca Maxwell Anderson, on 22 Aug 1895 in Kingsport, Tennessee. He was born on 13 May 1842 in Tennessee. He died on 29 Mar 1922 in Scott, Virginia.

vii. (13) JOSEPH SEVIER VANCE (page 25) was born on 28 Mar 1854 in Sullivan Co, Tennessee. He died on 5 Apr 1932 in Green Spring, Virginia. He married MAXIE MATILDA FAIN on 24 Aug 1882 in Hawkins County,Tennessee. She was born on 14 Aug 1862 in Hawkins County, Tennessee. She died on 24 Apr 1952 in Kingsport, Tennessee.

viii. JAMES HARVEY VANCE was born on 18 Dec 1857 in Sullivan County, Tennessee. He died on 29 Dec 1881 in Mississippi. He married MARGARET FOSTER TADLOCK on 10 May 1881. She was born on 9 Oct 1857. She died on 17 Jul 1896.

ix. JANE ISABEL VANCE was born on 28 Feb 1860 in Sullivan County, Tennessee. She died on 22 Feb 1888 in Kingsport, Tennessee.

5. DAVID GRAHAM VANCE (William Kirkpatrick[2], Dr. Patrick[1]) was born on 4 Oct 1812 in Jonesborough, Tennessee. He died on 26 Jan 1878 in Buford, Georgia. He married (1) MARY JANE MCCORKLE, daughter of John McCorkle and Mary "Polly" Cunningham, on 10 Jun 1834 in Washington County, Tennessee. She was born on 30 Jun 1816 in Tennessee. She died on 21 May 1859 in Greenville, Tennessee. He married (2) CATHARINE BRITTON, daughter of Major James Britton II and Margaret Pauline "Polly" Robinson, on 17 Nov 1859 in Greene County, Tennessee. She was born in 1821 in Greene County, Tennessee. Her death date is unknown: she was last seen in 1870 in Monroe County with the rest of the family. David is buried in Hillcrest Cemetery with many of his family. I have not been able to get to Georgia to look closer at the burials but was sent a number of photographs by a local named Dorsey Stancil so I cannot be sure that she is not buried in Buford.

The census of 1850 lists his occupation as Inn Keeper and he is living in the inn with his family. It states that he has real estate valued at $3500. He remarried within six months of Mary Jane's death in 1859. There were 7 children at home that next year with five under 13. The youngest, Edgar Walter, was only 3 when his mother died.

The decade following his father's decline and death in 1852 was one of real estate movement as he tried to configure his debt that he incurred when he bought the inn from his brothers. In 1859, it appears that he gave up and he sold to "William West, deed of trust for all real and personal property owned by David G. Vance. David indebted to several creditors for an amount in excess $5271.07. Wit: D.A. Kennedy; John M. Vance."[55] In other words he forfeited all property to get out from under the debt. Whether this was purely financial or preparing the upcoming war is not known.

The next year in 1860 David is listed in the census as a Master Saddler and James is an apprentice saddler. David's brother Patrick (saddler) was living with him as well. As there may have been an established saddler there in Greeneville already, they could have been working out of Sullivan County/Jonesboro where William K had a leather shop before as well as Greeneville.

East Tennessee was abolitionist and the center of that was Greeneville making the Civil War a time of real uncertainty for the Vance family. Though they were slave owners (only a few per household), maybe only one of them fought in the war. Slave ownership was never high in Tennessee. I found one source that said in 1860 only one person in the state had more than 300 slaves. (The author was Patton, page 22) That same source likens the ensuing years as a struggle between the wealthy and aristocratic classes versus the non-slaveholding classes in the rural and mountainous region. (Patton, 51) I have lost the book title, my apologies!

Were the Vances part of the wealthy aristocracy? Actually, the answer may be yes for David's two doctor brothers. Looking at the occupations and marriages for their children, the list reads like a who's who of Greeneville - lawyers, doctors and bankers. David, however was the exception. By the time the Civil War started, his finances appeared to be in disarray, his business dreams dashed and struggling to make a living for his large family . East Tennessee was virtually under martial law before 1862, occupied by the Confederate army. Up until 1863, David and his son, Wm K, were still buying and selling property. The draft was instituted in April of 1863 - and it specifically exempted tanners as well as doctors and lawyers. All saddlers were also tanners and the first orders reflecting selling to the army started in 1862.

The Vances were hard at work supplying the confederate army with saddles and bridles. I found 14 pay notices to David, his brother Patrick Henry, and his son, Wm K., for multiple orders in 1862 and 1863. One in Oct 1862 was for $5260.00, one in Dec 1862 for 2328.00 and one in Oct 1863 for $2350.00 were samples but some were as low as only $20. One was marked Greeneville; the larger orders were marked Abington, just across the Tennessee line in Virginia, and Goodson (Bristol). The last order was that one in Oct of 1863; November and December of that year saw the war brought home to Chattanooga and Knoxville.

Reconstruction was specially difficult for East Tennessee Confederates. Since David and his family actively worked with the army, they may have felt the need to leave Tennessee for their safety and to rebuild their lives. The story is really quite sad. If you are interested in what happened to the area during and after the war, I suggest getting a copy of W. Todd Groce's Mountain Rebels: East Tennessee Rebels and the Civil War, 1860-1870. It's a thorough examination and quite readable as well.

The 1870 census he and the family are on the move, living in Monroe

55. Greene County Book of Deeds 30:163.

County, about halfway down Tennessee towards Georgia. They may have felt safer there or they actually might have been traveling at the time. The 1870 census lists his occupation and his sons', John, James, David, Charles, occupations as saddler. They were living with a George Gennis (possibly not correct spelling as the census is not a good scan) age 70. That census is missing only William who was probably in Georgia already, Caroline (married, 1868) and Henry who was living nearby.

There is no question that David's oldest, William K, was in Georgia in the 1860s due to two Greene County deeds that said he was in Upson County and Columbus.

Since David died in Georgia in 1878, we know the family moved there by then. Buford started rapidly expanding in the early 1870s after the completion of the railroad in 1871 so they could have been there that early and I lean toward thinking that was the case.

The family Bible: "David Graham Vance departed this life on Saturday the 26th day of January 1778 at 9 1/2 Oclock A.M." That bible is in the hands of an Allen family member and includes notations that look to be recorded in my mother's handwriting of more recent deaths. Since Caroline Vance Foreman was working on the genealogy, the handwriting could also be hers (also educated in the same school system as my mother).

Mary Jane's grave inscription reads: "Sacred to the memory of Mary Jane Daughter of John & Mary McCorkle and consort of David G. Vance" From the family Bible: "Mary J M Vance departed this life on Saturday May 21st 1869 at 7 oclock P.M."

Father John McCorkle was also a saddler (census of 1860). Mary Jane's brother, Samuel, married another child (Margaret) of James Britton, lawyer and sheriff, the father of David's second wife, Catherine.

Catharine's first marriage to Lewis J Drake was performed by another McCorkle, Francis Allison McCorkle, the major Presbyterian minister.

I cannot find either Catharine or Edgar Walter, the youngest and my great-grandfather, in any census of 1880 together or singly.

David Graham Vance and Mary Jane McCorkle had the following children:
i.   WILLIAM KIRKPATRICK VANCE was born on 15 Mar 1835 in Greeneville, Tennessee, and died on 6 Jan 1884 in Tennessee. He married LOUISA C D WILSON on 22 May 1856 in Tennessee. She was born about 1837 in Virginia. He is missing from 1870 census and there is no information on Louisa after 1880 and nothing on their son, FRANCIS born 1857, after 1860. His 1880 residence is in Ooltewah, Tennessee, only 35 miles from Spring Place, Georgia, (near Dalton) where his brother Charles was living in 1880. There are various Tennessee deeds describing his Georgia purchases. The 1880 census says Louisa is disabled with epilepsy.
ii.   (14) JOHN MCCORKLE VANCE (page 26) was born on 20 Mar 1837 in Greeneville, Tennessee. He married N LOUISA PUCKETT on 8 Apr 1873 in Fulton County, Georgia. She was born about 1857 in Georgia and died before 1900 in Georgia.

iii. KEZIA ROBERTSON VANCE was born in 1838 in Greene County, Tennessee, and died in 1843 in Greene County, Tennessee.

iv. (15) JAMES HARVEY VANCE (page 26) was born on 27 Aug 1839 in Greeneville, Tennessee. He died before 1910 in Fulton County, Georgia. He married MARY ELIZABETH FLEMING on 17 Sep 1861 in Greenville, Tennessee. She was born on 1 Feb 1843 in Greene County, Tennessee, and died on 3 Feb 1914 in Fort Valley, Georgia.

v. (16) CAROLINE FLORENCE VANCE (page 27) was born in 1842 in Tennessee, and died on 10 Oct 1910 in Savannah, Georgia. She married JOHN TUNIS BEEKS in 1868. He was born in Jun 1836 in Indiana and died on 11 Aug 1904 in Savannah, Georgia (death certificate says he was a chemist).

vi. (17) CHARLES NICHOLAS VANCE (page 27) was born on 7 Aug 1845 in Greenville, Tennessee, and died on 14 Aug 1904 in Georgia. He married LOUISA JANE STAPLES on 14 Feb 1876. She was born on 25 Feb 1855 in Kentucky and died on 23 Sep 1928 in Birmingham, Alabama.

vii. MARY EMMA VANCE was born on 19 Nov 1847 in Greenville, Tennessee, and died on 4 Dec 1847 in Greenville.

viii. (18) DAVID FRANCIS VANCE (page 28) was born on 10 Apr 1849 in Greeneville, Tennessee, and died on 10 Feb 1933 in Gwinnett County, Georgia. He married LENORA VICTORIA "NORA" POOLE in Nov 1877 in Georgia. She was born on 27 Jan 1859 in Gwinnett County, Georgia, and died on 4 Apr 1943 in Georgia .

ix. (19) HENRY CLAY VANCE (page 28) was born on 15 Apr 1852 in Tennessee and died on 10 Jan 1891 in Florida. He married MARY VIRGINIA "JENNIE" JAMES on 18 Jul 1882 in Cumming, Georgia. She was born in Dec 1855 in Buford, Georgia, and died in 1911 in Jasper, Alabama.

x. (20) FANNIE M VANCE (page 29) was born on 20 Aug 1856 in Tennessee and died on 3 Jun 1947 in Buford, Georgia. She married JOSEPH D CHAPMAN in 1883. He was born on 8 May 1849 in Cassville, Georgia, and died in Mar 1933 in Buford, Georgia.

xi. (21) EDGAR WALTER VANCE (page 29) was born on 20 Nov 1857 in Greeneville, Tennessee and died on 26 Oct 1931 in Gwinnett, Georgia. He married CORA AMELIA ALLEN on 6 Jun 1883 in Gwinnett County, Georgia. She was born on 1 Apr 1866 in Georgia and died on 18 Aug 1949 in Gwinnett, Georgia.

6. WILLIAM NICHOLAS VANCE, MD, (William Kirkpatrick[2], Dr. Patrick[1]) was born on 12 Nov 1814 in Greeneville, Tennessee, and died on 12 Feb 1895 in Sullivan County, Tennessee. He married (1) SARAH ANNE NETHERLAND on 1 Oct 1839 in Kingsport, Tennessee. She was born on 28 Mar 1820 in Kingsport, Tennessee, and died on 13 Feb 1868 in Bristol, Tennessee (of consumption). He married (2) HELENA MCILWAINE on 15 Aug 1871 in County Cork, Ireland. She was born on 25 Dec 1850 in Ireland and died on 26 Mar 1882 in Sullivan County, Tennessee. He attended medical school at Transylvania University with his brother in 1833-34 but is not listed as graduating from that school.[56]

"Dr. Wm. Nicholas Vance after being several years a widower was married at the Cathedral of Cork in Ireland to his distant kinswoman Miss Helena Mcllwaine (notice change of spelling. of .McElwaine / Mcllwaine), youngest

---

56. per B J Gooch University Archivist, TU, Lexington, KY, email Sept 2015

*child of the late Mr. Joseph McIlwaine of Ballyr.onan Co., Londonderry ,
youngest son of Mr. Robert McIlwaine of Ballyrnilligan and Sarah Vance.
This Sarah Vance was sister to John Vance of Coagh , County Tyrone; to Joseph Vance of Cookstown, to Alderman James Vance, sometimes High Sheriff and Lord Mayor of Dublin and these 4 were cousins germain to General
Andrew Jackson, President United States whose mother Miss Vance was
sister to their father James Vance of Coagh, to Wm. Vance of Antrim and to
Andrew Vance who also emigrated to America." (Vance Family Association
files.)*

William Nicholas Vance and Sarah Anne Netherland had the following children:

i.   (22) KEZIAH ROBERTSON VANCE (page 30) was born on 8
      Sep 1840 in Kingsport, Tennessee, and died on 4 Apr 1916 in King-
      sport, Tennessee. She married Dr. GEORGE EDWARD PATTON
      on 26 Oct 1858 in Kingsport, Tennessee. He was born on 13 Dec
      1830 in Kingsport, Tennessee, and died on 24 May 1900 in King-
      sport.

ii.   (23) MARY H MOLLIE VANCE (page 31) was born on 7 Jul 1843
      in Kingsport, Tennessee and died on 24 Apr 1899 in Bristol, Ten-
      nessee. She married ELIJAH HILL SENEKER on 16 Mar 1880 in
      Goodson, Virginia. He was born on 9 Jul 1831 in Lee County, Vir-
      ginia, and died on 1 Jan 1917 in Johnson City, Tennessee.

iii. (24) SAMUEL NETHERLAND VANCE, (page 31) lawyer, was
      born on 21 Aug 1845 in Kingsport, Tennessee and died on 20 May
      1895 in Knoxville, Tennessee. He married BRIDGET AGNES FITZ-
      GERALD in Knoxville, Tennessee. She was born on 17 Mar 1855 in
      Virginia and died on 26 Nov 1921 in Knoxville, Tennessee.

iv.   (25) CHARLES SEVIER VANCE, MD, (page 31) was born on 20
      Aug 1847 in Kingsport, Tennessee and died on 10 Feb 1922 in John-
      son City, Tennessee. He married MARY ELIZABETH "MOLLIE"
      BRYAN in 1883. She was born on 21 Jun 1850 in Texas and died on
      17 Jun 1915.

v.   (26) ALICE VANCE (page 32) was born on 7 Nov 1849 in King-
      sport, Tennessee, and died on 7 Dec 1928 in Winchester, Kentucky.
      She married Rev ALEXANDER DOAK TADLOCK on 19 May 1876
      in Bristol, Tennessee. He was born on 27 May 1851 in Anderson,
      Tennessee, and died on 19 Dec 1928 in Winchester, Kentucky.

vi.   (27) WILLIAM KIRKPATRICK VANCE, MD, (page 33) was born
      on 27 May 1852 in Kingsport, Tennessee. He died on 29 Dec 1928
      in Bristol, Tennessee. He married MARIE SUZANNE DORIOT in
      1882. She was born on 17 Apr 1861 in Wytherville, Virginia, and
      died on 18 Apr 1948 in Bristol, Tennessee.

vii. IDA NETHERLAND VANCE was born on 26 Oct 1854 in Tennes-
      see and died on 21 Dec 1941 in Bristol, Tennessee. She married JO-
      SEPH ALEXANDER CALDWELL in Tennessee. He was born on 9
      Jan 1853 in Tennessee and died on 13 Jan 1914.

viii. JANE "JENNIE" VANCE was born on 19 Mar 1857 in Sullivan
      County, Tennessee and died on 27 Nov 1905 in Bristol, Tennessee.,

ix.   ROBERT NETHERLAND VANCE was born on 20 Feb 1859 in
      Sullivan County, Tennessee, and died on 23 Jul 1863 in Bristol,
      Tennessee.

William Nicholas Vance and Helena McIlwaine had the following children:

x.   HARRIETT "HATTIE" ELIZABETH VANCE was born on 17 Apr 1873 in Kingsport, Tennessee, and died in Apr 1976 in Bristol, Tennessee. She married FRANK ALEXANDER GROSECLOSE on 1 Dec 1908 in Sullivan County, Tennessee. He was born 28 Dec 1874 in Virginia and died 23 May 1954 in Bristol, Tennessee. They had VANCE BALBIRNIE GROSECLOSE, born 28 Nov 1909 in Bristol, Tennessee, died 24 Feb 1991. He married MARY ELIZABETH ROBINSON, born 20 Oct 1906, died 18 Feb 1974 in Bristol, Virginia.

xi.   (28) CHARLOTTE LENOX VANCE (page 33) was born on 8 Jul 1878 in Greeneville, Tennessee. She died on 8 Jul 1931 in Washington, D.C. (from being run over by an automobile). She married WILLIAM BASCOM POWERS. He was born on 18 Jan 1875 in Virginia. He remarried and died 1967 in Virginia.

7.   CAROLINE FLORENCE VANCE (William Kirkpatrick[2], Dr. Patrick[1]) was born on 7 Nov 1822 in Greeneville, Tennessee. She died on 7 Dec 1881 in Cleveland, Tennessee. She married PLEASANT M CRAIGMILES, a banker from Cleveland, on 17 Jan 1843 in Greene County, Tennessee. He was born on 4 Oct 1813 in Tennessee and died on 8 Sep 1876 in Cleveland, Tennessee.

Pleasant M Craigmiles and Caroline Florence Vance had the following children:
i.   (29) AUGUSTA C CRAIGMILES (page 34) was born in Aug 1846 in Tennessee, and died on 24 Dec 1931 in Berkeley, California. She married THOMAS MELMOTH OSMENT on 27 Nov 1872 in Bradley, Tennessee. He was born in 1841 in Tennessee and died on 20 Dec 1905 in San Francisco, California.

ii.   FANNIE CRAIGMILES was born on 17 Dec 1850. She died on 24 Jul 1854.

iii.   WALTER CRAIGMILES was born on 21 Feb 1855 in Tennessee and died on 3 Oct 1928 in Chattanooga, Tennessee. He married ANNIE SANDUSKY on 3 Nov 1881. She was born on 1 May 1862 in Cleveland, Tennessee, and died on 19 Aug 1891 in Cleveland, Tennessee. They had one son: PLEASANT MILLER CRAIGMILES was born on 23 Jan 1883 in Cleveland, Tennessee, and died on 5 Nov 1913 in Shelbyville, Tennessee.

iv.   FRANCES CAMPBELL CRAIGMILES b. 29 Mar 1858 d. 7 Mar 1862 in Tennessee.

v.   EDWARD CRAIGMILES b. 21 May 1861 d. 27 Mar 1862.

8.   KEZIAH P "KIZZIE" VANCE (William Kirkpatrick[2], Dr. Patrick[1]) was born on 10 Dec 1825 in Washington County, Tennessee and died on 17 Nov 1902 in Knox County, Kentucky. She married Dr. OLIVER PERRY HERNDON on 2 Mar 1846 in Washington County, Tennessee. He was born on 4 Apr 1826 in Cumberland Ford, Kentucky, and died on 17 Jul 1897 in Barbourville, Kentucky.

Oliver Perry Herndon and Keziah P "Kizzie" Vance had the following children:
i.   RICHARDSON HERNDON was born on 8 Feb 1847 in Knox County, Kentucky, and died on 23 Mar 1862 in Knox.

ii.   WILLIAM HERNDON was born on 9 May 1848 in Barbourville, Kentucky, and died on 16 Feb 1933 in Jacksonville, Florida.

iii.   (30) JAMES VANCE HERNDON (page 34) was born in Feb 1850 in Knox County, Kentucky, and died on 20 Nov 1939 in Hunt, Texas. He married HESTER ANNE DIXON in 1875 in Texas. She was born in Feb 1855 in Springfield, Missouri, and died on 17 Sep 1920 in Kaufman, Texas.

iv. JANE HERNDON was born on 1 Feb 1852 in Knox, Kentucky. She died on 24 Dec 1870 in Knox.

v. (31) BENJAMIN FRANKLIN HERNDON, MD, (page 34) was born on 9 Jul 1853 in Knox, Kentucky. He died on 24 Feb 1929 in Danville, Kentucky. He married SALLIE J BALL. She was born in Jan 1850 in Kentucky and died on 1 Sep 1930 in Boyle, Kentucky.

vi. (32) FLORENCE "FLORA" CAROLINE HERNDON (page 34) was born on 24 Apr 1858 in Knox County, Kentucky. She died on 14 Feb 1919 in Barbourville, Kentucky. She married (1) WILLIAM B ANDERSON on 15 May 1877 in Knox. He was born on 13 Feb 1824 in Knox County, Kentucky, and died on 10 Mar 1901 in Barbourville, Kentucky. She married (2) DAVID C PAYNE on 30 Oct 1912 in Knox County.

vii. (33) THOMAS R. HERNDON (page 35) was born about 1859 in Knox County, Kentucky and died on 11 Dec 1915 in Greeneville, Texas. He married ANNIE in 1882. She was born in Mar 1866 in Tennessee.

viii. ALEXANDER "ALEX" NIELSON HERNDON was born on 17 May 1860 in Barbourville, Kentucky, and died on 15 Oct 1929 in Barbourville, Kentucky, He married MARGARET TINSLEY on 10 Jan 1883 in Barbourville, Kentucky. She was born on 10 Jan 1860 in Kentucky and died on 6 Jan 1940 in Knox County, Kentucky.

ix. (34) CHARLES GLEASON HERNDON, MD, (page 35) was born on 23 Aug 1861 in Barbourville, Kentucky. He died on 20 Oct 1903. He married MAGGIE J DISHMAN on 8 Oct 1890 in Knox County, Kentucky. She was born on 3 Sep 1886 in Kentucky and died on 6 Oct 1887 in Kentucky.

x. JOHN E HERNDON was born on 21 Jul 1866 in Barbourville, Kentucky and died on 18 Aug 1884 in Barbourville, Kentucky.

xi. GEORGE F HERNDON was born on 21 Jul 1866 in Barbourville, Kentucky, and died on 7 Feb 1893 in St, Louis, Missouri.

9. HARRIET GRAHAM VANCE (William Kirkpatrick[2], Dr. Patrick[1]) was born on 31 May 1829 in Greene County, Tennessee. She died on 27 Nov 1926 in Dallas, Texas. She married PLEASANT LAWSON THORNTON. He was born on 5 Nov 1831 in Georgia and died on 4 Mar 1907 in Grayson County, Texas. He was a farmer from the Dalton area of Georgia, just south of the Tennessee border. He did fight in the civil war and she received a pension after his death. He was in company F, 12th Regiment, Georgia Cavalry.

Pleasant Lawson Thornton and Harriet Graham Vance had the following children:

i. (35) PATRICK HENRY THORNTON (page 36) was born on 13 Jan 1855 in Murray County, Georgia, and died on 20 Jul 1913 in Dallas, Texas. He married FRANCIS ELLEN CRISP in 1883. She was born on 4 Mar 1852 in Arkansas and died on 15 Mar 1919 in Dallas, Texas.

ii. SUSAN THORNTON b. 13 Nov 1856 in Georgia d. 18 Apr 1862.

iii. FANNIE THORNTON was born on 15 May 1860 in Tennessee and died on 3 Mar 1924 in Dallas, Texas. She married a MCFADDEN.

iv.   ALICE THORNTON was born on 21 May 1861 in Tennessee and died on 9 Jul 1955 in Highland Park, Dallas County, Texas. She married a JACKSON.

v.   RAYMOND THORNTON b. about 1865 in Georgia d. before 1880.

vi.   WALTER VANCE THORNTON was born on 16 Sep 1868 in Bradley County, Tennessee, and died on 6 Jan 1930 in Oklahoma. He married MARGARET E. who was born in Illinois about 1873.

10.   SUSAN N VANCE (William Kirkpatrick[2], Dr. Patrick[1]) was born in 1833 in Tennessee and died on 30 Mar 1873 in Sullivan County, Tennessee. She married JAMES STROTHER PATTON in 1850. He was born on 19 Oct 1827 in Kingsport, Tennessee, and died on 28 Jun 1903 in Kingsport, Tennessee.

James Strother Patton and Susan N Vance had the following children:

i.   WILLIAM KIRKPATRICK PATTON was born in 1851 in Sullivan County, Tennessee, and died in 1870 (lost without trace on visit to Texas).

ii.   (36) FLORENCE CAROLINE PATTON (page 36) was born in 1854 in Tennessee and died before 1883. She married GORDON WILLIAM JORDAN on 14 Sep 1873 in Sullivan,Tennessee. He was born about 1851 in Tennessee and died before 1905 in Knoxville, Tennessee.

Generation 4

11.   CHARLES ROBERTSON VANCE, lawyer, (James Harvey[3], William Kirkpatrick[2], Dr. Patrick[1]) was born on 22 Aug 1835 in Cherokee, Tennessee. He died on 12 Nov 1911 in Bristol, Tennessee. He married MARGARET JANE NEWLAND, daughter of Joseph Newland Jr. and Rebecca Maxwell Anderson, on 16 Oct 1860 in Arcadia, Tennessee. She was born on 28 Mar 1838 in Arcadia, Tennessee, and died on 8 Apr 1914 in Bristol, Tennessee. He was a prominent lawyer and read law with Hon. Thomas A.R. Nelson from 1856-1858. After admittance to the bar he ran for attorney-general of his district in Kingsport. He first enlisted as a private but contracted typhoid. He then served as a Captain during the civil war, taking and reporting claims for property damaged or destroyed. He was indicted for treason at the end of the war but case was dismissed on the payment of costs. He was the attorney for the East Tennessee, Virginia and Georgia railroad. He was a whig before the war and a democrat afterwards. He owned a farm (140 acres) just outside of Bristol. He attended Rogersville and Rutherford Academies and Washington College. Lived at Estilville after the war for three years as a refuge. He served as President of the Board of Trustees of King College for 20 years. (I apologize but after writing these notes, I failed to record where I found this information.)

Charles Robertson Vance and Margaret Jane Newland had the following children:

i.   (37) Rev JAMES ISAAC VANCE was born on 25 Sep 1862 in Arcadia, Tennessee and died on 24 page 36Nov 1939 in Blowing Rock, North Carolina. He married MAMIE STILES CURRELL on 22 Dec 1886. She was born in 1862 in Yorkville, South Carolina, and died about 1945 in Nashville, Tennessee.

ii.   (38) JOSEPH ANDERSON VANCE, DD, (page 37) was born on

17 Nov 1864 in Arcadia, Tennessee, and died in 1946. He married MARY BAXTER FORMAN on 15 Jan 1890 in Chicago, Illinois. She was born on 21 Oct 1866 in Maysville, Kentucky, and died on 9 Aug 1943 in Detroit, Michigan.

iii. CHARLES ROBERTSON VANCE Jr was born on 1 Oct 1867 in Gate City, Virginia, and died on 26 Feb 1947 in Bristol, Tennessee. He married SARAH TREAT LYMAN on 1 Oct 1896 in Norfolk, Virginia. She was born on 12 Aug 1870 in Ohio and died on 17 Jan 1954 in Bristol, Tennessee.

iv. MARGARET "MAGGIE" JANE VANCE was born on 9 Dec 1869 in Gate City, Virginia, and died on 30 Oct 1943 in Bristol, Tennessee.

v. (39) REBEKAH MALINDA "REBA" VANCE (page 38) was born on 20 Jan 1874 in Bristol, Tennessee, and died on 7 Apr 1949 in Bristol, Tennessee. She married CHARLES LUTHER DUNN HEDRICK on 9 Oct 1897 in Bristol, Tennessee. He was born on 7 May 1869 in Tazewell, Virginia, and died on 21 Dec 1920 in Bristol.

12. WILLIAM V VANCE, lawyer (James Harvey[3], William Kirkpatrick[2], Dr. Patrick[1]) was born in 1848 in Sullivan County, Tennessee. He died before 1900 in Tennessee. He married MARY FRANCIS "FANNIE" MILLER b.1848 on 15 Sep 1869 in Hawkins, Tennessee.

William V Vance and Mary Francis Miller had the following children:

i. SAMUEL VANCE was born about 1871 in Tennessee.

ii. OLIVER VANCE was born about 1873 in Tennessee. May be the same as boy Vance below.

iii. ANNIE F. VANCE was born about 1874 in Tennessee. She died in 1950.

iv. BOY VANCE was born in Feb 1880 in Union, Tennessee.

v. (40) IDA BELLE VANCE (page 38) was born on 5 Nov 1882 in Bristol, Tennessee, and died on 18 Dec 1946 in Bristol, Tennessee. She married WILLIAM RILEY STONE, Jr. He was born on 2 Aug 1876 in Tennessee, and died on 15 Jul 1940 in Bristol, Tennessee.

13. JOSEPH SEVIER VANCE (James Harvey[3], William Kirkpatrick[2], Dr. Patrick[1]) was born on 28 Mar 1854 in Sullivan County, Tennessee. He died on 5 Apr 1932 in Green Spring, Virginia. He married MAXIE MATILDA FAIN on 24 Aug 1882 in Hawkins, Tennessee. She was born on 14 Aug 1862 in Hawkins County, Tennessee, and died on 24 Apr 1952 in Kingsport, Tennessee.

Joseph Sevier Vance and Maxie Matilda Fain had the following children:

i. (41) CHARLES RUTLEDGE VANCE (page 39) was born on 27 Jun 1885 in Tennessee and died in 1960 in Tennessee. He married LULA BURL WARRICK. She was born on 14 Nov 1888 in Lincoln, West Virginia, and died on 2 Apr 1970 in Tennessee.

ii. (42) ELIZABETH "BESS" LYONS VANCE (page 39) was born in 1887 in Tennessee. She married WILLIAM SAMUEL PIERCE. He was born on 16 Apr 1879 in Tennessee and died on 6 Jun 1966 in Tennessee.

iii. JAMES FOSTER VANCE was born in 1887. He died before 1888.

iv. (43) SAMUEL FAIN VANCE (page 39) was born on 17 Jun 1893 in Tennessee. He died on 20 Sep 1975 in Hopewell, Virginia. He married TOMMIE ADELINE CARROLL. She was born about 1902 in Tennessee and died in St. Petersburg, Florida.

14. JOHN MCCORKLE VANCE (David Graham[3], William Kirkpatrick[2], Dr. Patrick[1]) was born on 20 Mar 1837 in Greeneville, Tennessee. He married N LOUSIA PUCKETT on 8 Apr 1873 in Fulton County, Georgia. She was born about 1857 in Georgia and died before 1900 in Georgia. In 1900 John is living next door to his future son-in-law in Athens, Georgia. Their house was situated close to the corner of Cedar St and S. Lumpkin but that is now UGA campus and there are no houses on S. Lumpkin any longer.

John McCorkle Vance and N Louisa Puckett had the following children:
   i.   JOHN A VANCE was born about 1877 in Georgia.
   ii.   (44) REBECCA "BECCA" VANCE (page 39) was born on 17 Dec 1882 in Georgia and died on 12 Sep 1970 in Madison, Georgia. She married MARTIN LUTHER VAN WINKLE, Sr, on 9 Jan 1901 in Athens, Georgia. He was born on 14 Mar 1871 in Patterson, New Jersey, and died in 1940 in Georgia.
   iii. FRED VANCE was born in Jun 1884 in Georgia.
   iv.   EDDIE VANCE was born in Aug 1888 in Georgia.

15. JAMES HARVEY VANCE (David Graham[3], William Kirkpatrick[2], Dr. Patrick[1]) was born on 27 Aug 1839 in Greeneville, Tennessee, and died before 1910 in Fulton County, Georgia. He married MARY ELIZABETH FLEMING on 17 Sep 1861 in Greenville, Tennessee. She was born on 1 Feb 1843 in Greene County, Tennessee, and died on 3 Feb 1914 in Fort Valley, Georgia. He disappears from the census before 1910 where Mary is living near Calhoun with David and her grandson. The deaths records for that decade may not be available at all. I have not found his grave though on-the-ground exploration of the Buford Cemetery may well find him.

James Harvey Vance and Mary Elizabeth Fleming had the following children:
   i.   (45) DAVID NELSON VANCE (page 40) was born on 25 Feb 1864 in Tennessee and died in Georgia. He married LILLIE B BYERS on 17 Mar 1889 in Gwinnett County, Georgia.
   ii.   WALTER E VANCE was born in Sep 1866 in Tennessee. He died on 24 Dec 1936 in Atlanta, Georgia. He married LEILA ESPY, daughter of John Ferdinand Espy and Mary Allen, about 1891. She was born in Jan 1872 in Georgia. Mary Allen was the daughter of Washington Allen - original ancestor of all the Allens connected with the Vances.
   iii. (46) CHARLES H VANCE (page 40) was born about 1868 in Tennessee and died in 1936 in Georgia. He married TALLULAH LAVANIA HENDRIX in 1890. She was born in Jul 1868 in Georgia and died on 12 Apr 1948 in Fulton County, Georgia.
   iv.   JOHN FLEMING VANCE was born on 16 Jun 1868 in Tennessee and died on 4 Jan 1870 in Tennessee.
   v.   (47) FRANK ARMSTRONG VANCE (page 40) was born on 7 Jan 1872 in Georgia and died on 6 Dec 1941 in Fort Valley, Georgia. He married JANE MAXWELL SHEPHERD on 2 Feb 1910 in Houston, Georgia. She was born on 3 Nov 1889 in Georgia and died on 17 Oct 1986 in Fort Valley, Georgia.
   vi.   (48) JAMES FLEMING VANCE (page 41) was born on 30 Jul 1876 in Georgia and died on 28 Sep 1950 in Montgomery, Alabama. He married MILDRED B BROOKS. She was born on 10 Jul 1881 in Georgia and died on 19 May 1945 in Selma, Alabama.

vii. (49) Rev EDGAR MCGAUGHEY VANCE (page 41) was born on 12 Jan 1879 in Belton, Georgia, and died on 16 Jul 1947 in Glynn County, Georgia. He married SUE GERALDINE WALKER on 12 Nov 1902 in Clarkesville, Georgia. She was born on 7 Apr 1881 in Augusta, Georgia, and died on 26 Sep 1970 in Huntington Beach, California.

viii. (50) ERNEST WORD VANCE (page 42) was born on 22 Apr 1882 in Rome, Georgia. He died on 10 Mar 1951 in Eufaula, Alabama. He married LUCIA ARNOLD EDWARDS on 7 Aug 1906 in Houston, Georgia. She was born on 10 Mar 1886 in Perry, Georgia, and died on 24 Dec 1977 in Eufaula, Alabama.

ix. (51) JOHN BOYD VANCE (page 42 was born on 21 Dec 1886 in Georgia and died on 2 Oct 1967 in Fort Valley, Georgia. He married OLA BEALE HARWELL. She was born on 14 Mar 1885 in Georgia and died on 10 May 1976 in Fort Valley, Georgia.

16. CAROLINE FLORENCE VANCE (David Graham[3], William Kirkpatrick[2], Dr. Patrick[1]) was born in 1842 in Tennessee and died on 10 Oct 1910 in Savannah, Georgia. She married JOHN TUNIS BEEKS in 1868. He was born in Jun 1836 in Indiana and died on 11 Aug 1904 in Savannah, Georgia (death certificate says he was a chemist). EW Vance was her executor/ administrator (her brother). I think Fannie may have died at the same time but I did find a possible marriage record in Indiana for Fanny to a Anson Gillewall.

John Tunis Beeks and Caroline Florence Vance had the following children:

i. MARY CORNELIA BEEKS was born on 21 Oct 1868 in Greenville, Tennessee. She died on 13 Apr 1910 in Savannah, Georgia. She married VAN HORTEN before 1907 in Savannah, Georgia.

ii. FANNIE V BEEKS was born on 18 Dec 1874 in Fort Wayne, Indiana.

17. CHARLES NICHOLAS VANCE (David Graham[3], William Kirkpatrick[2], Dr. Patrick[1]) was born on 7 Aug 1845 in Greenville, Tennessee, and died on 14 Aug 1904 in Georgia. He married LOUISA JANE STAPLES on 14 Feb 1876. She was born on 25 Feb 1855 in Kentucky. She died on 23 Sep 1928 in Birmingham, Alabama.

Charles Nicholas Vance and Louisa Jane Staples had the following children:

i. CHARLES ROY VANCE was born on 19 Mar 1877 in Dalton, Georgia, and died on 23 Apr 1948 in Carter, Tennessee. He married CLETA MAY STAPLES on 24 May 1911 in Sebastian, Arkansas. She was born on 13 Jul 1894 in Boones Creek, Tennessee, and died on 30 Jun 1982 in Avery County, North Carolina.

ii. DAVID FREDERICK VANCE was born on 28 Jan 1879 in Georgia. He died on 10 Dec 1916 in Dalton, Georgia.

iii. MILLIE BROOK VANCE was born on 10 Jul 1881 in Georgia.

iv. JOHN HENRY VANCE was born on 3 Apr 1883 in Springplace, Georgia. He died on 12 Mar 1958 in Prob. Selma, Alabama. He married AUDREY EUGENIA MCFERRIN about 1910 in Dallas County, Alabama. She was born on 26 Aug 1889 in Alabama and died on 8 Dec 1971 in Selma, Alabama.

v. (52) CLARENCE LUCIAN VANCE (page 42 was born on 2 Jul 1886 in Georgia and died on 25 Oct 1957. He married EDNA MAE ELUM on 6 May 1910 in Cincinnati, Ohio. She was born on 12 Mar 1892 in Ohio and died on 26 Mar 1954 in Birmingham, Alabama.

vi. (53) MARY INEZ VANCE (page 42) was born on 4 Aug 1888 in

Georgia. She married HARVEY GORDON KNOTT. He was born on 23 Oct 1890 in Georgia and died on 6 Mar 1936 in Lynchburg, Virginia.

vii. (54) NICHOLAS ROUSSEAU VANCE (page 43) was born on 10 Feb 1892 in Georgia. He died on 16 Oct 1955 in Birmigham, Alabama. He married MARGARET LOUISE "SUG" DULION. She was born on 5 Jun 1903 in Alabama and died on 12 Dec 1976 in Birmingham, Alabama.

viii. MARTHA FLORENCE VANCE was born on 12 Apr 1897 in Georgia and died on 18 Jul 1990.

18. DAVID FRANCIS VANCE (David Graham[3], William Kirkpatrick[2], Dr. Patrick[1]) was born on 10 Apr 1849 in Greeneville, Tennessee. He died on 10 Feb 1933 in Gwinnett County, Georgia. He married LENORA VICTORIA "NORA" POOLE in Nov 1877 in Georgia. She was born on 27 Jan 1859 in Gwinnett County, Georgia, and died on 4 Apr 1943 in Georgia.

David Francis Vance and Lenora Victoria "Nora" Poole had the following children:

i. NENA LENORA VANCE was born on 13 Sep 1878 and died on 22 Jun 1959 in Hall County, Georgia.

ii. (55) OSCAR FRANCIS VANCE page 43) was born on 18 Nov 1880 in Georgia and died on 15 Aug 1958 in Bibb County, Georgia. He married ELIZABETH LUCY B REESE on 17 Dec 1914 in Houston County, Georgia. She was born on 6 Aug 1882 in Thomasville, Georgia, and died on 21 Sep 1968 in Macon, Georgia.

iii. ETHEL MARY VANCE was born on 18 Feb 1883 and died on 12 Jun 1958 in Gwinnett County, Georgia.

iv. ROBERT EARLE VANCE was born in Jul 1886 in Buford, Georgia, and died on 20 Apr 1959 in Gainesville, Georgia. He married ANNE IRENE RANKIN on 20 Jul 1935. She was born on 20 Aug 1904 in Georgia and died on 20 Jan 1995 in Gainesville, Georgia.

v. GRAHAM ATTICUS VANCE was born on 2 Nov 1888 in Georgia and died on 22 Dec 1893 in Georgia.

vi. CAROLYN VANCE was born on 21 Sep 1896 in Gwinnett County, Georgia, and died on 7 May 1982 in Buford, Georgia. She married LAUREN WOOD FOREMAN in 1951. He was born on 9 May 1880 in Georgia and died in Feb 1966 in Buford, Georgia.

vii. BABY VANCE was born about 1905 in Georgia.

viii. ADELAIDE POOLE VANCE was born on 10 Jan 1905 in Georgia and died on 29 Apr 1956. She married THOMAS WESLEY MORGAN. He was born on 15 May 1914 in Georgia and died on 16 Mar 1975 in Atlanta, Georgia.

19. HENRY CLAY VANCE (David Graham[3], William Kirkpatrick[2], Dr. Patrick[1]) was born on 15 Apr 1852 in Tennessee and died on 10 Jan 1891 in Florida. He married MARY VIRGINIA "JENNIE" JAMES on 18 Jul 1882 in Cumming, Georgia. She was born in Dec 1855 in Buford, Georgia, and died in 1911 in Jasper, Alabama.

Henry Clay Vance and Mary Virginia "Jennie" James had the following children:

i. (56) FLORENCE ELIZABETH VANCE (page 43) was born on 14 Oct 1884 in Georgia and died in Apr 1975 in Jasper, Alabama. She married CHARLES LELLARD BURTON in 1905 in Gwinnett County, Georgia. He was born on 25 Oct 1882 in Georgia and died on 15 Dec 1952 in Jasper, Alabama.

ii. JAMES VANCE was born on 2 Apr 1888 and died on 29 Aug 1888 in Florida.

iii. (57) HENRY CLAY VANCE, Jr, (page 44) was born on 12 Dec 1890 in Orlando, Florida, and died in Dec 1963 in Alabama. He married ALICE VIRGINIA GORDON before 1912 in Birmingham, Alabama. She was born on 11 Jan 1893 in Alabama and died on 30 Dec 1973 in Birmingham, Alabama.

20. FANNIE M VANCE (David Graham[3], William Kirkpatrick[2], Dr. Patrick[1]) was born on 20 Aug 1856 in Tennessee. She died on 3 Jun 1947 in Buford, Georgia. She married JOSEPH D CHAPMAN in 1883. He was born on 8 May 1849 in Cassville, Georgia, and died in Mar 1933 in Buford, Georgia.

Joseph D Chapman and Fannie M Vance had the following children:

i. ESSIE CHAPMAN was born on 18 Jun 1882 in Georgia and died on 19 Apr 1982 in McDonough, Georgia. She married WALTER B BROGDON. He was born on 22 Aug 1880 in Georgia and died on 23 May 1958.

ii. FLORENCE CHAPMAN was born about 1883 in Georgia.

iii. (58) JOSEPH VANCE CHAPMAN (page 44) was born on 30 Jun 1888 in Georgia and died on 23 Nov 1971 in Tuscumbia, Alabama. He married ANNE SMITH KEYS on 3 Nov 1919 in Tuscumbia, Alabama. She was born on 16 Aug 1899 in Tuscumbia, Alabama, and died on 2 Aug 1988 in Tuscumbia.

21. EDGAR WALTER VANCE (David Graham[3], William Kirkpatrick[2], Dr. Patrick[1]) was born on 20 Nov 1857 in Greeneville, Tennessee. He died on 26 Oct 1931 in Gwinnett, Georgia. He married CORA AMELIA ALLEN in 1882 in Gwinnett County, Georgia. She was born on 1 Apr 1866 in Georgia and died on 18 Aug 1949 in Gwinnett, Georgia. Her father was Robert H Allen who had the first harness shop in Buford in 1868, a year after he moved there. It was his brother, Bonaparte Allen, who started the Bona Allen Tanning Company which gave rise to the large and profitable Allen enterprises. The most complete description I found online was this: http://www.aboutnorthgeorgia.com/ang/Bona_Allen_Tannery. There are several histories of Buford so I assume there is more information in print. If anyone gets to Buford, I'm sure there is a wealth of information available at the Museum and in the local library. My mother has a picture of him in his goat cart.

Edgar Walter Vance and Cora Amelia Allen had the following children:

i. EMMA MAE VANCE was born on 5 Jun 1884 in Georgia and died on 8 Mar 1922 in Shelbyville, Tennessee. She married IVAN LONG POWER on 30 Apr 1912 in Buford, Georgia. He was born on 4 Nov 1879 in Georgia and died on 17 Dec 1962 in Shelbyville, Tennessee.

ii. (59) CORA ALLINE VANCE (page 44) was born on 24 Jun 1886 in Buford, Gwinnett County, Georgia, and died on 5 Feb 1975 in Buford, Georgia. She married (1) HORACE WADLEIGH ALLEN, son of Bonaparte "Bona" Allen Sr and Louisa Jane Stanley, on 26 Apr 1904 in Buford, Georgia. He was born on 9 May 1886 in Buford, Georgia. He died on 15 Feb 1920 in Buford, Georgia. She married (2) Dr JAMES GRIFFIN WILLIAMS about 1921. He was born on 8 Dec 1885 in Alexandria, Louisiana, and died on 9 Aug 1968 in Atlanta, Georgia.

iii. (60) ROBERT GRAHAM VANCE (page 45) was born on 9 Dec

1892 in Buford, Georgia, and died on 23 Jun 1959 in Gainesville, Georgia. He married MAMIE NEIL ELAM. She was born on 7 Apr 1899 in South Carolina and died on 26 Feb 1996 in Gainesville, Georgia.

iv. EDGAR ALLEN VANCE was born on 15 Feb 1899 in Georgia and died on 16 Nov 1955 in Lookout Mountain, Tennessee. He married EULALEE CHEEK, daughter of John Samuel Cheek and Cora, on 15 Jul 1924 in Hall, Georgia (Per Michael R Allen). She was born about 1903 in Georgia and died on 1 Jan 1961.

22. KEZIAH ROBERTSON VANCE (William Nicholas[3], William Kirkpatrick[2], Dr. Patrick[1]) was born on 8 Sep 1840 in Kingsport, Tennessee. She died on 4 Apr 1916 in Kingsport, Tennessee. She married Dr GEORGE EDWARD PATTON on 26 Oct 1858 in Kingsport, Tennessee. He was born on 13 Dec 1830 in Kingsport, Tennessee, and died on 24 May 1900 in Kingsport, Tennessee.

George Edward Patton Dr and Keziah Robertson Vance had the following children:

i. (61) SAMUEL N PATTON, MD, (page 45) was born on 17 Oct 1859 in Kingsport, Tennessee and died on 11 Jul 1923 in Kingsport, Tennessee. He married (1) ELLEN A LESLIE in Tennessee. She was born on 28 Mar 1861 and died on 5 Sep 1890 in Kingsport,Tennessee. He married (2) OCTAVIA MOORE after 1890. She was born on 16 May 1874 in Virginia and died on 7 May 1975 in Kingsport, Tennessee.

ii. WILLIAM NICHOLAS PATTON II was born on 6 Sep 1861 in Kingsport, Tennessee, and died on 25 Feb 1928 in Macon, Georgia (auto wreck returning from Florida). He married NANCY "ANNIE" NETHERLAND on 5 Oct 1889 in Kingsport, Tennessee. She was born on 5 Oct 1866 in Kingsport, Tennessee, and died on 28 Feb 1968 in Arcadia, Florida.

iii. (62) HENRY EUGENE PATTON (page 46) was born on 1 Feb 1863 in Kingsport, Tennessee, and died on 17 May 1947 in Bristol, Virginia. He married (1) EMMA SHOWWALTER on 26 Oct 1884 in Tennessee. She was born in 1869 in Tennessee and died on 7 Sep 1885 in Kingsport, Tennessee. He married (2) DELORES "DOLLIE" ALTONIA CRUMLEY in 1886. She was born on 18 Oct 1867 in Tennessee and died on 18 Aug 1953 in Bristol, Virginia.

iv. (63) MARY FRANCES PATTON (page 46) was born on 16 Oct 1865 in Kingsport, Tennessee, and died on 6 Oct 1954 in New Orleans, Louisiana. She married GEORGE WILLIAM SCHULTZ. He was born in Sep 1861 in Germany and died about Feb 1943.

v. GEORGE EDWARD PATTON, Jr, was born on 17 Oct 1867 in Kingsport, Tennessee, and died on 28 Jul 1869 in Kingsport, Tennessee.

vi. SYDNEY E PATTON was born on 27 Oct 1869 in Kingsport, Tennessee, and died on 2 Jun 1870 in Kingsport, Tennessee.

vii. ANNIE PATTON was born on 15 Sep 1871 in Kingsport, Tennessee, and died on 30 May 1872 in Kingsport, Tennessee.

viii. (64) ALBERTA "BERTIE" PATTON (page 47 was born on 27 Nov 1873 in Kingsport, Tennessee, and died on 2 May 1918 in Louisville, Kentucky. She married BENJAMIN BARKER KELLY in 1890. He was born on 3 Feb 1872 in Louisville, Kentucky, and died on 15 Dec 1942 in Louisville, Kentucky.

ix. (65) CHARLES VANCE PATTON (page 47) was born on 9 Sep

1876 in Tennessee, and died on 6 Oct 1964 in Knoxville, Tennessee. He married (1) BONNIE BOYER. She died in Nov 1875. He married (2) AMANDA DUCKWORTH. She was born on 4 Oct 1892 in Tennessee and died in Jul 1977 in Tennessee.

   x.   (66) NANNIE ROSE PATTON page 48 was born on 6 Apr 1880 in Kingsport, Tennessee, and died on 24 Apr 1964 in Kingsport, Tennessee. She married BENJAMIN RICHARD CLOUD on 8 Nov 1901 in Kingsport, Tennessee. He was born on 10 Nov 1877 in Kingsport and died on 20 Mar 1939 in Kingsport.

   xi.   (67) VICTOR PATTON (page 48) was born on 13 Mar 1884 in Kingsport, Tennessee, and died on 27 Dec 1973 in Kingsport. He married (1) ELIZABETH HEATHERLY on 10 Apr 1959 in Tulare, California. She was born on 20 Feb 1887 in Lafollette County, Tennessee, and died on 30 Jan 1971 in Kingsport. He married (2) REATA LORRAINE POWELL. She was born on 11 Jun 1883 in Tennessee and died on 8 Dec 1955 in Kingsport, Tennessee.

   xii.   HERMAN PATTON was born on 4 May 1886 in Kingsport, Tennessee and died on 17 Dec 1969 in Kingsport.

23.   MARY H "MOLLIE" VANCE (William Nicholas[3], William Kirkpatrick[2], Dr. Patrick[1]) was born on 7 Jul 1843 in Kingsport, Tennessee, and died on 24 Apr 1899 in Bristol, Tennessee. She married ELIJAH HILL SENEKER on 16 Mar 1880 in Goodson, Virginia. He was born on 9 Jul 1831 in Lee County Virginia, and died on 1 Jan 1917 in Johnson City, Tennessee.

Elijah Hill Seneker and Mary H Mollie Vance had the following children:

   i.   (68) MARY VANCE SENEKER (page 49 was born on 20 Jul 1881 in Goodson, Virginia, and died on 27 Dec 1959 in Kansas City, Missouri. She married ERNEST LOCKE HODGE on 4 Feb 1903 in Bristol, Virginia. He was born on 6 May 1874 in Missouri and died on 25 Nov 1950.

   ii.   ANDREW SENEKER was born on 19 Apr 1883 in Tennessee and died on 4 Oct 1895 in Tennessee.

   iii.   (69) HUGH HILL SENEKER (page 49) was born on 11 Dec 1884 in Bristol, Virginia, and died on 16 Feb 1952 in Topeka, Kansas. He married ETHEL B GILMORE, born about 1891 in Missouri.

   iv.   EDGAR HENDERSON SENEKER was born on 22 Feb 1887 in Virginia and died on 28 Jul 1909 in Bismarck, North Dakota.

24.   SAMUEL NETHERLAND VANCE, lawyer (William Nicholas[3], William Kirkpatrick[2], Dr. Patrick[1]) was born on 21 Aug 1845 in Kingsport, Tennessee, and died on 20 May 1895 in Knoxville, Tennessee. He married BRIDGET AGNES FITZGERALD in Knoxville, Knox, Tennessee. She was born on 17 Mar 1855 in Virginia and died on 26 Nov 1921 in Knoxville, Knox, Tennessee. One of his descendants, Kathy Manning, writes: "Sam Vance was baptized a Catholic Nov. 15, 1877, and they married on Nov. 20, 1877. According to my dad, Sam's law partners immediately dissolved the firm. I think this was also the reason my family did not have a relationship with the rest of the Vance family--when I saw an old Vance family tree filed in the historical collection here, and they gave Bridget's maiden name as Kirkpatrick, I thought good lord they didn't even know her well enough to get her last name right. These trees usually say "no further information" (on children, etc.), as though the family had just dropped off the face of the earth."
Another mention spoke of the Sam's family being ostracized.

Samuel Netherland Vance and Bridget Agnes Fitzgerald had the following children:

i. (70) WILLIAM NICHOLAS VANCE (page 49) was born on 25 Aug 1880 in Knoxville, Tennessee, and died on 20 Dec 1939 in Knoxville. He married LAURA E JACKSON. She was born about 1890 in Tennessee.

ii. AMELIUS JOSEPH VANCE was born in 1881 in Tennessee. He died in 1900 in Tennessee.

iii. CHARLES EDWARD VANCE was born on 16 Sep 1881 in Knoxville, Tennessee. He died in Alabama.

iv. (71) DAVID ANDERSON VANCE (page 49) was born on 4 Apr 1882 in Tennessee and died on 10 Jun 1938 in Tarrant, Texas. He married BLANCHE LEE CHRISTIAN on 24 Aug 1903 in Fannin, Texas. She was born on 7 Sep 1886 in Kentucky and died on 4 Jun 1978 in Silver City, New Mexico.

v. PATRICK H VANCE was born in Sep 1886 in Morgan, Tennessee, and died on 16 Apr 1912 in Lenoir City, Tennessee (killed in a accident on the railroad).

vi. (72) MARY NETHERLAND VANCE (page 50) was born on 4 Dec 1886 in White Sulphur Springs, Virginia, and died on 10 Dec 1944 in Knoxville, Tennessee. She married JOHN JOSEPH MANNING, Jr. He was born on 8 Nov 1869 in Knoxville, Tennessee, and died on 18 Nov 1939 in Knoxville.

vii. (73) LILLIAN F "LEE" VANCE (page 50) was born on 26 Jun 1888 in Wartburt, Tennessee, and died on 17 Jul 1966 in Charleston, South Carolina. She married JOHN ALOYSIOUS MILTON. He was born on 21 Jun 1887 in Chattanooga, Tennessee, and died on 3 Jul 1939 in Knoxville, Tennessee.

viii. (74) SAMUEL NETHERLAND VANCE (page 51) was born on 15 Jun 1890 in Tennessee and died on 24 Mar 1937 in Knoxville, Tennessee. He married MAUD AGNES BARNITZ. She was born on 7 Jul 1892 in Tennessee and died on 4 Nov 1976 in Tennessee.

ix. JOSEPHINE VANCE b. 1891 in Tennessee, d. 1899 in Tennessee.

25. CHARLES SEVIER VANCE, MD, (William Nicholas[3], William Kirkpatrick[2], Dr. Patrick[1]) was born on 20 Aug 1847 in Kingsport, Tennessee, and died on 10 Feb 1922 in Johnson City, Tennessee. He married MARY ELIZABETH "MOLLIE" BRYAN in 1883. She was born on 21 Jun 1850 in Texas and died on 17 Jun 1915.

Charles Sevier Vance Dr and Mary Elizabeth "Mollie" Bryan had the following child:

i. MOLLIE VANCE was born in May 1880 in Texas.

26. ALICE VANCE (William Nicholas[3], William Kirkpatrick[2], Dr. Patrick[1]) was born on 7 Nov 1849 in Kingport, Tennessee, and died on 7 Dec 1928 in Winchester, Kentucky. She married Rev ALEXANDER DOAK TADLOCK on 19 May 1876 in Bristol, Tennessee. He was born on 27 May 1851 in Anderson, Tennessee, and died on 19 Dec 1928 in Winchester, Kentucky. He was the first president of King College in Briston, Tennessee.

Alexander Doak Tadlock and Alice Vance had the following children:

i. EDWIN VANCE TADLOCK REV was born on 2 Jan 1878 in Greenup OR Carter, Kentucky. He died in 1941 in Sarasota, Florida. He married MARY B BARTHOLOMEW. She was born in 1883 in West

Virginia and died after 1957.

ii.   JAMES THORNWELL TADLOCK was born on 19 Apr 1881 in Kentucky and died on 15 Nov 1963 in Bourbon, Kentucky. He married LUCY JANE WEATHERS. She was born on 4 Feb 1882 in Bourbon County, Kentucky, and died on 13 Jul 1961 in Bourbon, Kentucky.

27.   WILLIAM KIRKPATRICK VANCE, MD, (William Nicholas[3], William Kirkpatrick[2], Dr. Patrick[1]) was born on 27 May 1852 in Kingsport, Tennessee. He died on 29 Dec 1928 in Bristol, Tennessee. He married MARIE SUZANE DORIOT in 1882. She was born on 17 Apr 1861 in Wytheville, Virginia, and died on 18 Apr 1948 in Bristol, Tennessee.

Dr. William Kirkpatrick Vance and Marie Suzanne Doriot had the following children:
i.   (75) FREDERICK VICTOR VANCE, Sr, (page 51) was born on 18 Feb 1888 in Sullivan County, Tennessee, and died on 19 Dec 1976 in Bristol, Tennessee. He married (1) MARY HELEN GRAY in 1918 in Wytheville, Virginia. She was born on 13 Dec 1897 in Illinois and died on 26 Jun 1957 in Bristol, Tennessee. He married (2) YOLANDE HENDERSON. She was born on 5 Oct 1896.
ii.   WILLIAM KIRKPATRICK "DICK" VANCE, MD, was born on 6 Nov 1889 in Sullivan County, Tennessee. He died in Aug 1977 in Bristol, Tennessee. He married INEZ SNYDER. She was born on 16 Feb 1898 in North Carolina and died 15 Jun 1994.
iii.   MARIE DORIOT VANCE was born on 30 Aug 1891 and died on 18 Jul 1895 (of meningitis).
iv.   DAVID GRAHAM VANCE was born on 30 Dec 1894 in Bristol, Tennessee, and died on 27 Oct 1918 in USNAS Eastleigh, England (flu / pneumonia).
v.   (76) DOUGLAS DORIOT VANCE, MD, (page 51) was born on 31 Jan 1896 in Tennessee and died on 4 Apr 1989 in Sullivan County, Tennessee. He married KATHERINE VIRGINIA MILLNER on 24 Sep 1930 in Norfolk, Virginia. She was born on 5 Jan 1902 in Norfolk County, Virginia, and died on 30 Sep 1995 in Bristol, Virginia.
vi.   KATHLEEN BALBIRNIE VANCE b. 6 Sep 1897 d. 11 Sep 1897.

28.   CHARLOTTE LENOX VANCE (William Nicholas[3], William Kirkpatrick[2], Dr. Patrick[1]) was born on 8 Jul 1878 in Greenville, Tennessee. She died on 8 Jul 1931 in Washington, D.C. (from being run over by an automobile). She married WILLIAM BASCOM POWERS. He was born on 18 Jan 1875 in Virginia.

William Bascom Powers and Charlotte Lenox Vance had the following children:
i.   HERMAN LENOX POWERS was born on 13 Jan 1906 in Tennessee and died on 29 May 1917 in Johnson City, Tennessee.
ii.   (77) LYNN HUNTLEY POWERS (page 52) was born on 18 Mar 1909 in Bristol, Tennessee and died on 21 Dec 2008 in Cleveland, Ohio. He married (1) GOLDIE B BRYAN. She was born on 18 Sep 1910 in Tennessee. and died on 31 Jul 1987 in Ohio. He married (2) MAUDE ELIZABETH BRICKER on 20 May 1989 in Bristol, Virginia.
iii.   HELENA MCILWAINE POWERS b. 11 Mar 1919 d. 26 Aug 1923 in Johnson City, Tennessee.

29. AUGUSTA C CRAIGMILES (Caroline Florence[3], William Kirkpatrick[2], Dr. Patrick[1]) was born in Aug 1846 in Tennessee and died on 24 Dec 1931 in Berkeley, California. She married THOMAS MELMOTH OSMENT on 27 Nov 1872 in Bradley, Tennessee. He was born in 1841 in Tennessee and died on 20 Dec 1905 in San Francisco, California.

Thomas Melmoth Osment and Augusta C Craigmiles had the following children:

    i.   (78) VANCE CRAIGMILES OSMONT, Sr, (page 52) was born on 3 May 1874 in Cleveland, Tennessee, and died on 8 Feb 1943 in Piedmont, California. He married MARY PIERCE HALL on 2 Apr 1908 in Alameda, California. She was born on 29 Jun 1876 in San Francisco, California, and died on 23 May 1960 in California.

    ii.   (79) ADELIA R OSMENT (page 52) was born on 26 Oct 1876 in Tennessee and died on 20 Feb 1971 in Alameda, California. She married JAMES CLARENCE SPERRY. He was born on 18 Sep 1874 in California and died on 20 Nov 1942 in Alameda County, California.

30. JAMES VANCE HERNDON (Keziah P[3], William Kirkpatrick[2], Dr. Patrick[1]) was born in Feb 1850 in Kentucky and died on 20 Nov 1939 in Hunt, Texas. He married HESTER ANNE DIXON in 1875 in Texas. She was born in Feb 1855 in Springfield, Missouri, and died on 17 Sep 1920 in Kaufman County, Texas.

James Vance Herndon and Hester Anne Dixon had the following children:

    i.   JOHNNY HERNDON was born about 1872 in Texas.

    ii.   (80) OLIVER PERRY HERNDON (page 53) was born on 12 Apr 1876 in Greenville, Texas, and died on 16 Jan 1945 in Dallas, Texas. He married LULA GRAHAM on 2 Apr 1900 in Greenville, Texas. She was born on 6 Apr 1880 in Missouri and died on 26 Feb 1977 in Plano, Texas.

    iii.   (81) LENA H HERNDON (page 53) was born on 23 Dec 1880 in Sherman, Texas, and died on 23 Dec 1978 in Greenville, Texas. She married JOHN BEAUCHAMP on 27 Jun 1900 in Hunt, Texas. He was born on 30 Apr 1875 in Dallas, Texas, and died on 29 Oct 1927 in Sherman, Texas.

31. BENJAMIN FRANKLIN HERNDON, MD, (Keziah P[3], William Kirkpatrick[2], Dr. Patrick[1]) was born on 9 Jul 1853 in Knox, Kentucky, and died on 24 Feb 1929 in Danville, Kentucky. He married SALLIE J BALL. She was born in Jan 1850 in Kentucky and died on 1 Sep 1930 in Boyle, Kentucky.

Benjamin Franklin Herndon and Sallie J Ball had the following child:

    i.   (82) MILDRED HERNDON (page 53) was born on 21 Mar 1883 in McLennan County, Texas,and died on 19 May 1913 in Waco, Texas. She married CHARLES JAMES MCKINLEY about 1904 in Texas. He was born on 5 Aug 1877 in Limestone County, Texas, and died on 1 Jun 1960 in Trinidad, Colorado.

32. FLORENCE "FLORA" CAROLINE HERNDON (Keziah P[3], William Kirkpatrick[2], Dr. Patrick[1]) was born on 24 Apr 1858 in Kentucky and died on 14 Feb 1919 in Barbourville, Kentucky. She married 1) WILLIAM B ANDERSON on 15 May 1877 in Knox. He was born on 13 Feb 1824 in Kentucky, and died on 10 Mar 1901 in Barbourville, Kentucky. She married (2) DAVID C PAYNE on 30 Oct 1912 in Knox County.

William B Anderson and Florence "Flora" Caroline Herndon had the following children:

i. (83) WILLIAM B ANDERSON (page 54) was born 20 Mar 1862 in Knox County, Kentucky, and died 2 Dec 1920 in Fayette, Kentucky. (A revenue agent murdered. His killer was never found.) He married AMANDA "MANNIE" CHINN in 1888 in Lexington, Kentucky. She was born in Jul 1870 in Kentucky. She died on 15 Nov 1939 in Lexington, Kentucky.

ii. NANCEY B ANDERSON was born about 1873 in Kentucky.

iii. (84) FINLEY BOYD ANDERSON (page 54) was born on 16 Jan 1875 in Barbourville, Kentucky, and died on 30 Jun 1949 in Conway, Arkansas. He married FLO VIVIAN LEEK. She was born on 17 Apr 1884 in Missouri and died on 11 Aug 1969 in Orange City, California.

iv. (85) VICTOR VANCE ANDERSON, MD, (page 54) was born on 26 Dec 1878 Kentucky and died in 1960 in Hyde Park, New York. He married (1) MARGARET C before 1906. She was born on 12 Jul 1896 in Ohio and died in Aug 1984 in Staatsburg, New York. He married (2) CLARA B SMITH in 1906. She was born 18 Jan 1881 in Louisiana. She died 28 Jan 1928.

33. THOMAS RENFRO HERNDON (Keziah P[3], William Kirkpatrick[2], Dr. Patrick[1]) was born about 1859 in Kentucky and died on 11 Dec 1915 in Greeneville, Texas. He married ANNIE in 1882. She was born on 16 Mar 1868 in Tennessee and died on 21 Nov 1948.

Thomas R Herndon and Annie had the following children:

i. FLORA HERNDON was born in 14 Jun 1887 in Kentucky and died 23 Feb 1940.

ii. (86) MARY HERNDON (page 55) was born in 19 Oct 1889 in Kentucky and died 2 Dec 1977. She married SIDNEY RUFUS PONDER. He was born 14 Feb 1879 in Calhoun, Georgia, and died 23 Jun 1953 in Ft. Worth, Texas.

iii. LILLIE VANCE HERNDON was born in 27 Jun 1893 in Kentucky and died 30 Jan 1982.

iv. ALEXANDER HERNDON was born 11 Sep 1898 in Kentucky and died 25 Feb 1918.

v. JAMES HERNDON was born about 1904 in Texas.

34. CHARLES GLEASON HERNDON MD (Keziah P[3], William Kirkpatrick[2], Dr. Patrick[1]) was born on 23 Aug 1861 in Barbourville, Kentucky, and died on 20 Oct 1903. He married MAGGIE J DISHMAN on 8 Oct 1890 in Kentucky. She was born on 3 Sep 1886 in Kentucky and died on 6 Oct 1887 in Knox County, Kentucky.

Charles Gleason Herndon and Maggie J Dishman had the following children:

i. DANIEL HARVEY HERNDON, MD, was born on 23 Jul 1891 in Kentucky and died on 26 Aug 1971 in Barbourville, Kentucky. He married STUART MILLER on 11 Sep 1919 in Kentucky. She was born on 1 Oct 1899 in Kentucky and died on 31 May 1964 in Kentucky.

ii. BENJAMIN C HERNDON was born on 26 Dec 1893 in Kentucky and died 22 Sep 1954 in Barbourville. He married MODELL RUSSELL on 11 Dec 1917 in Faulkner, Arkansas. She was born about 1899 in West Virginia.

35. PATRICK HENRY THORNTON (Harriet Graham Vance[3], William Kirkpatrick[2], Dr. Patrick[1]) was born on 13 Jan 1855 in Murray County, Georgia, and died on 20 Jul 1913 in Dallas, Dallas County, Texas. He married FRANCES ELLEN CRISP in 1883. She was born on 4 Mar 1852 in Arkansas and died on 15 Mar 1919 in Dallas, Texas.

Patrick Henry Thornton and Francis Ellen Crisp had the following children:
   i.   ALICE THORNTON was born in Apr 1883 in Arkansas.
   ii.   JOHN CRISP THORNTON was born on 6 Dec 1884 in Mount Holly, Arkansas. He died on 31 May 1965 in Dallas, Texas.
   iii. (87) IRENE THORNTON (page 55) was born on 15 May 1888 in Hope, Arkansas, and died on 3 Jul 1953 in Houston, Texas. She married (1) SIDNEY CLAY WILKES. He was born on 7 Sep 1885 in Kosse, Texas, and died on 21 Sep 1958 in Galveston, Texas. She married (2) THEODORE LAWSON LUTHER. He was born about 10 Oct 1860 in Cassville, Georgia, and died 17 Apr 1942 in Dallas, Texas.

36. FLORENCE CAROLINE PATTON (Susan N Vance[3], William Kirkpatrick[2], Dr. Patrick[1])was born in 1854 in Tennessee and died before 1883. She married GORDON WILLIAM JORDAN on 14 Sep 1873 in Sullivan,Tennessee. He was born about 1851 in Tennessee and died before 1905 in Knoxville, Tennessee.

Gordon William Jordan and Florence Caroline Patton had the following children:
   i.   HUGH KIRK JORDAN was born on 15 Aug 1874 in Montgomery County,Virginia, and died on 5 Jan 1945 in Los Angeles, California. He married NANCY "NANNIE" ADKINS on 28 Jan 1905 in Knox, Tennessee. She was born in 1887.
   ii.   HATTIE JORDAN was born about 1876 in Montgomery County,-Virginia.
   iii. PERRY EVERETT JORDAN was born about 1878 in Montgomery County,Virginia.

Generation 5

37. Rev JAMES ISAAC VANCE (Charles Robertson[4], James Harvey[3], William Kirkpatrick[2], Dr. Patrick[1]) was born on 25 Sep 1862 in Arcadia, Tennessee, and died on 24 Nov 1939 in Blowing Rock, North Carolina. He married MAMIE STILES CURRELL on 22 Dec 1886. She was born in 1862 in Yorkville, South Carolina, and died about 1945 in Nashville, Tennessee. He graduated Kings College and the Union Theological Seminary in Virginia.

The Rev. James Isaac Vance succeeded the venerable and honored Dr. Armstrong, having been installed pastor 1st October, 1891. Mr. Vance is the son of Charles R. Vance, Esq , of Bristol, Tennessee, an attorney in that city, and a ruling elder in the First Presbyterian Church. He was born 25th September, 1862. He is of Scotch-Irish extraction, and his people have been Presbyterians for generations. On his father's side he is closely related to John Sevier, a hero of Revolutionary fame, and first governor of the State of Tennessee. Mr. Vance received his classical education at King College, Bristol, Tennessee, from which institution he was graduated in 1883. He obtained his theological education at Union Theological Seminary in Virginia, graduating from that institution in 1886. He was ordained and installed pastor of the church of Wytheville by the Presbytery of Abingdon in May, 1886, and on 1st December, 1887, he took charge of the Second Presbyterian Church of Alexandria. From this charge, where his labors had been specially blessed in large accessions to the membership, in increased liberality, and in the spirit of harmony and Christian zeal cultivated and developed, he has come under peculiarly auspicious circumstances to the First Presbyterian Church of Norfolk. In this church, the labors of a year have been signally blessed also, and in like particulars. Mr. Vance is a man of fine presence, rich, strong voice, and impressive delivery. His sermons are clear and forceful, abounding in effective illustration. His social qualities, and his ability as an organizer, make him attractive to the young, and give promise of great usefulness. Mr. Vance was married in 1886 to Miss Currell of South Carolina, sister of Dr. W. S. Currell, professor in Davidson College, North Carolina.[57]

James Isaac Vance and Mamie Stiles Currell had the following children:

i. MARGARET VANCE was born on 5 Feb 1888 in Alexandria, Virginia, and died on 20 Nov 1972 in Blowing Rock, North Carolina.

ii. (88) WILLIAM CURRELL VANCE, Sr, (page 55) was born in Jul 1889 in Alexandria, Virginia, and died in 1965 in Nashville, Tennessee. He married NELLA PATTERSON. She was born in 1891 in Pennsylvania and died in 1954 in Washington, D.C.

iii. (89) AGNES WILKIE VANCE (page 56) was born on 4 Jul 1893 in Bristol, Tennessee, and died on 18 Aug 1963. She married ALLEN DOUGLAS BERRY. He was born on 12 May 1891 in Nashville, Tennessee, and died on 7 May 1960.

iv. (90) RUTH ARMSTRONG VANCE (page 56) was born on 2 Dec 1894 in Norfolk, Virginia, and died on 28 Jan 1958 in Nashville, Tennessee. She married GEORGE WIMBERLY KILLEBREW II on 8 Apr 1920 in Virginia. He was born on 8 Jul 1894 in Mount Pleasant, Tennessee, and died on 9 Jul 1958 in Nashville, Tennessee.

v. JAMES ISAAC VANCE, Jr, was born 11 May 1898 in Nashville, Tennessee, and died as an infant.

vi. (91) CHARLES ROBERTSON VANCE, Sr, (page 57) was born on 27 Nov 1899 in Nashville,Tennessee, and died on 4 Jan 1963 in Greensboro, North Carolina. He married MAURINE MOORE on 24 Feb 1925 in Guilford, North Carolina. She was born on 18 May 1902 in Guilford County, North Carolina, and died on 1 Aug 1987 in Greensboro, North Carolina.

38. JOSEPH ANDERSON VANCE, DD, (Charles Robertson[4], James Harvey[3], William Kirkpatrick[2], Dr. Patrick[1]) was born on 17 Nov 1864 in Arcadia, Tennessee. He may have died in 1946 in Michigan but I can find no proof of that. He married MARY BAXTER FORMAN on 15 Jan 1890 in Chicago, Illinois. She was born on 21 Oct 1866 in Maysville, Kentucky, and died on 9 Aug 1943 in Detroit, Michigan. He graduated Kings College and the Union Theological Seminary. He is the one who applied for the DAR.

Joseph Anderson Vance and Mary Baxter Forman have no living descendants but had the following children:

---

57. https://www.findagrave.com/cgi-bin/fg.cgi?page=gr&GRid=94084644

i. ROBERT F VANCE was born between 1890-1896. He died on 8 Aug 1896.

ii. DOROTHY VANCE was born on 14 Nov 1894 in Baltimore, Maryland, and died on 12 Oct 1967. She married JOHN M BONBRIGHT on 11 Jun 1931 in Detroit, Michigan. He was born about 1885 in Pennsylvania and died on 22 Dec 1972 in Detroit, Michigan.

iii. JOSEPH ANDERSON VANCE, Jr, was born on 6 Dec 1898 in Baltimore, Maryland, and died on 28 Jan 1978 in Detroit, Michigan. He married JEANNE M GILCHRIST on 19 Sep 1931 in Alpena, Michigan. She was born about 1908 in Michigan. They had one daughter, JEANNE GILCHRIST "JINNY" born 11 Oct 1935 in Detroit, Michigan and died 15 Dec 2003 in Lake Worth, Florida.

iv. MARY FORMAN VANCE was born on 1 Sep 1900 in Chicago, Illinois. She died on 29 Nov 1983 in Howell, Michigan. She married ORVILLE EDWARD REED on 16 Oct 1926 in Chicago, Illinois. He was born on 3 Apr 1899 in Terra Alta, Preston, West Virginia, and died on 19 Dec 1972 in Howell, Michigan. They had one daughter, MARY VIRGINIA REED born on 22 Jun 1932 in Michigan. She died on 16 Oct 2010 in Delaware County, Ohio. She was the principal researcher for the Patrick Vance family for years.

39. REBEKAH MALINDA "REBA" VANCE (Charles Robertson[4], James Harvey[3], William Kirkpatrick[2], Dr. Patrick[1]) was born on 20 Jan 1874 in Bristol, Tennessee, and died on 7 Apr 1949 in Bristol, Tennessee. She married CHARLES LUTHER DUNN HEDRCIK on 9 Oct 1897 in Bristol. He was born on 7 May 1869 in Tazewell, Virgina, and died on 21 Dec 1920 in Bristol.

Charles Luther Dunn Hedrick and Rebekah Malinda "Reba" Vance had the following children:

i. (92) MARGARET LETITIA HEDRICK (page 57) was born on 19 May 1900 in Bristol, Tennessee. She died on 6 Dec 1983 in Bristol, Tennessee. She married WILLIAM WASHINGTON NICKLES, Sr, on 20 Jun 1922 in Sullivan, Tennessee. He was born on 2 May 1900 in Bristol and died on 19 Sep 1961 in Bristol.

ii. MARY REBEKAH HEDRICK was born on 3 Nov 1905 in Bristol, Tennessee, and died on 20 Mar 1998 in Bristol.

40. IDA BELLE VANCE (William V[4], James Harvey[3], William Kirkpatrick[2], Dr. Patrick[1]) was born on 5 Nov 1882 in Bristol, Tennessee, and died on 18 Dec 1946 in Bristol, Tennessee. She married WILLIAM RILEY STONE, Jr. He was born on 2 Aug 1876 in Tennessee, and died on 15 Jul 1940 in Bristol, Tennessee.

William Riley Stone Jr and Ida Belle Vance had the following children:

i. (93) WILLIAM JAMES STONE (page 57) was born about 1904 in Bristol, Tennessee, and died about 1960 in Bristol, Tennessee. He married MARGARET "PEGGY" CHILDRESS on 4 Aug 1928 in Monroe, Tennessee. She was born about 1909 in Tennessee.

ii. (94) RILEY VANCE STONE (page 57) was born on 25 Dec 1906 in Tennessee and died on 22 Jul 1959 in Bristol, Tennessee. He married MARTHA AUGUSTA HORTON about 1927. She was born on 6 Dec 1907 in North Carolina and died on 4 May 1991 in Bristol, Virginia.

iii. JOHN WESTLEY "JACK" STONE was born on 1 Nov 1908 in Tennessee and died on 5 Apr 1955 in Bristol, Tennessee.

iv. MARY ANNA STONE was born on 28 Mar 1913 in Bristol, Tennessee and died on 16 Jan 1998 in Bristol, Tennessee. She married HARRY LEE SENTER. He was born on 16 Feb 1911 in Tennessee and died on 24 Mar 1981 in Bristol.

v. (95) IDA JANE STONE (page 58) was born on 5 Jun 1919 in Bristol, Tennessee, and died on 5 Feb 2009 in Bristol, Tennessee. She married HOMER AUGUSTUS JONES, Jr, on 23 Jun 1942. He was born on 23 May 1920 in Bristol, Tennessee, and died on 23 Jan 2011 in Bristol.

41. CHARLES RUTLEDGE VANCE (Joseph Sevier[4], James Harvey[3], William Kirkpatrick[2], Dr. Patrick[1]) was born on 27 Jun 1885 in Tennessee and died in 1960 in Tennessee. He married LULA BURL WARRICK. She was born on 14 Nov 1888 in Lincoln, West Virginia, and died on 2 Apr 1970 in Tennessee.

Charles Rutledge Vance and Lula Burl Warrick had the following children:
i. (96) ETHEL LOUISE VANCE (page 58) was born on 17 Mar 1911 in Tennessee. She died on 31 May 1996 in Harrisburg, Pennsylvania. She married W M RUSS.
ii. JOSEPH L VANCE was born on 16 Dec 1916 in Tennessee. He died on 21 Nov 1943 in Tarawa, Gilbert Islands, Kiribati. He married MARGARET ANN MILLARD. She was born on 7 Jun 1924 in Matewan, West Virginia. She died on 25 Apr 2006.

42. ELIZABETH "BESS" LYONS VANCE (Joseph Sevier[4], James Harvey[3], William Kirkpatrick[2], Dr. Patrick[1]) was born in 1887 in Tennessee. She married WILLIAM SAMUEL PIERCE. He was born on 16 Apr 1879 in Tennessee and died on 6 Jun 1966 in Tennessee.

William Samuel Pierce and Elizabeth "Bess" Lyons Vance had the following child:
i. (97) WILLIAM V PIERCE (page 58) was born on 27 Oct 1905 in Tennessee and died on 16 May 1981 in Kingsport, Tennessee. He married MYRTLE MCDONALD. She was born on 24 Apr 1909 in Wyoming and died on 29 Dec 1996 in Kingsport, Tennessee.

43. SAMUEL FAIN VANCE (Joseph Sevier[4], James Harvey[3], William Kirkpatrick[2], Dr. Patrick[1]) was born on 17 Jun 1893 in Tennessee and died on 20 Sep 1975 in Hopewell, Virginia. He married TOMMIE ADELINE CARROLL. She was born about 1902 in Tennessee. She died in St. Petersburg, Florida.

Samuel Fain Vance and Tommie Adeline Carroll had the following children:
i. JOSEPH CARROLL VANCE was born on 2 Feb 1922 in Louisa, Virginia, and died on 1 Dec 1998 in Fredericksburg, Virginia. He married JEAN CARTER SMITH on 6 Jun 1953 in Charlottesville, Virginia. She was born on 25 Sep 1923 in Williamson, West Virginia. She died on 22 Mar 1997.
ii. ELIZABETH E VANCE was born about 1923 in Virginia.
iii. ANN VANCE was born about 1929 in Virginia.

44. REBECCA "BECCA" VANCE (John McCorkle[4], David Graham[3], William Kirkpatrick[2], Dr. Patrick[1]) was born on 17 Dec 1882 in Georgia and died on 12 Sep 1970 in Madison, Georgia. She married MARTIN LUTHER VAN WINKLE, Sr, on 9 Jan 1901 in Athens, Georgia. He was born on 14 Mar 1871 in Patterson, New Jersey, and died in 1940 in Georgia.

Martin Luther Van Winkle Sr and Rebecca "Becca" Vance had the following

children:
i. (98) MARTIN "MR RIP" VAN WINKLE, Jr, (page 58) was born on 24 Aug 1903 in Georgia and died on 4 Jan 1998 in Pine Lake, Georgia. He married HATTILU ADAMS. She was born in 1905 in Georgia and died in 1998.
ii. HELEN LOUISE VAN WINKLE was born in 1907 in Georgia and died in 1971 in Georgia. She married GUNN.

45. DAVID NELSON VANCE (James Harvey[4], David Graham[3], William Kirkpatrick[2], Dr. Patrick[1]) was born on 25 Feb 1864 in Tennessee. He died in Georgia. He was last seen in Selma, Alabama, in 1930 (the giveaway is his occupation as harness maker.) He married LILLIE B BYERS on 17 Mar 1889 in Gwinnett County, Georgia. She died before 1900, possibly in childbirth.

David Nelson Vance and Lillie B Byers had the following child:
i. (99) HERMES HEZZION VANCE (page 59) was born on 2 Aug 1894 in Buford, Georgia, and died on 14 Jul 1950 in Los Angeles, California. He married NELL LAWRENCE. She was born on 13 Feb 1899 in Ohio and died on 23 Mar 1947 in Los Angeles County, California.

46. CHARLES H VANCE (James Harvey[4], David Graham[3], William Kirkpatrick[2], Dr. Patrick[1]) was born about 1868 in Tennessee. He died in 1936 in Georgia. He married TALLULAH LAVANIA HENDRIX in 1890. She was born in Jul 1868 in Georgia and died on 12 Apr 1948 in Fulton County, Georgia.

Charles H Vance and Tallulah Lavania Hendrix had the following children:
i. (100) ROY HENDRIX VANCE (page 59) was born on 2 Sep 1889 in Georgia. He died on 31 Jan 1973 in Buford, Georgia. He married ANDY ELIZABETH COBB on 16 Nov 1914 in Milton, Georgia. She was born on 6 Nov 1897 in Old Milton - Cherokee, GA. She died on 11 Jan 1955 .
ii. (101) LEONE VANCE (page 59) was born in Aug 1898 in Georgia and died on 1 Nov 1955 in Fulton County, Georgia. She married (1) ELLSWORTH CARTER SIMMONS on 14 Nov 1917 in Fulton, Georgia. He was born on 19 Oct 1896 in Arabi, Georgia, and died on 6 Sep 1977 in Volusia, Florida. She married (2) HARRY CLIFFORD LYON, MD. He was born on 14 May 1906 in Georgia and died on 27 Dec 1980 in Roswell, Georgia.
iii. CHARLES H VANCE was born on 12 Apr 1904 in Georgia. He died on 19 Feb 1905 in Georgia.
iv. WINFRED R VANCE was born on 21 May 1909 in Georgia. He died on 20 Apr 1965 in Richmond, Georgia. His WWII enlistment says he was married.

47. FRANK ARMSTRONG VANCE (James Harvey[4], David Graham[3], William Kirkpatrick[2], Dr. Patrick[1]) was born on 7 Jan 1872 in Georgia and died on 6 Dec 1941 in Fort Valley, Georgia. He married JANE MAXWELL SHEPHERD on 2 Feb 1910 in Houston, Georgia. She was born on 3 Nov 1889 in Georgia and died on 17 Oct 1986 in Fort Valley, Georgia.

Frank Armstrong Vance and Jane Maxwell Shepard had the following children:
i. FRANCES E VANCE was born on 21 Oct 1910 in Georgia. She died

on 5 May 1982 in Georgia. She married JOSEPH WARREN KIN-
NEY. He was born on 26 Jul 1905 and died on 29 Mar 1987 in Leon,
Florida.

ii.   (102) SARA ELIZABETH VANCE (page 59) was born on 22 Oct
      1913 in Georgia. She died on 11 Jun 2012 in Bradenton, Florida.
      She married GERALD LATCHAW CARNER. He was born on 28
      Feb 1912 in Georgia. He died on 23 Nov 2005 in Deland, Florida.

48. JAMES FLEMING VANCE (James Harvey[4], David Graham[3], William
     Kirkpatrick[2], Dr. Patrick[1]) was born on 30 Jul 1876 in Georgia and died
     on 28 Sep 1950 in Montgomery, Alabama. He married MILDRED B
     BROOKS. She was born on 10 Jul 1881 in Georgia and died on 19 May
     1945 in Selma, Alabama. His social security application lists Mary F Mc-
     Corkle as his mother. I can find no evidence that Mary was married to a
     McCorkle and it does look like she was born a Fleming. His death certifi-
     cate does list Mary Fleming instead.

James Fleming Vance and Mildred B Brooks had the following children:
i.   JAMES NICHOLAS VANCE was born on 8 Feb 1904 in Buford,
      Georgia, and died on 11 Mar 1948 in Selma, Alabama. He married
      KATHERINE LEE JACKSON. She was born on 22 Jul 1913 in Gal-
      veston, Texas, and died on 12 Nov 1948 in Selma, Dallas, Alabama.
ii.   FRANCES FLEMING VANCE was born about 1909 in Georgia.
iii. EDWARD STAPLES VANCE was born on 24 Jan 1915 in Selma,
      Alabama, and died on 9 Aug 1943 in Verbena, Alabama.
iv.   (103) ERNEST HOWARD VANCE (page 60) was born on 17 Dec
      1917 in Alabama. He died on 4 Apr 1962 in Dade County, Florida.
      He married HELEN M GOOLSBY. She was born on 21 May 1924
      and died on 21 Apr 2003.

49. Rev EDGAR MCGAUGHEY VANCE (James Harvey[4], David Graham[3],
     William Kirkpatrick[2], Dr. Patrick[1]) was born on 12 Jan 1879 in Belton,
     Georgia, and died on 16 Jul 1947 in Glynn County, Georgia. He married
     SUE GERALDINE WALKER on 12 Nov 1902 in Clarkesville, Georgia.
     She was born on 7 Apr 1881 in Augusta, Georgia, and died on 26 Sep
     1970 in Huntington Beach, California.

Edgar McGaughey Vance and Sue Geraldine Walker had the following children:
i.   MARY ELIZABETH VANCE was born on 10 Jan 1904 in Georgia
      and died on 7 Feb 1984 in Long Beach, California.
ii.   (104) PHILLIP TRENHOLM VANCE (page 60) was born on 16
      Feb 1906 in Georgia and died on 23 Nov 1978 in Port Angeles,
      Washington. He married DOROTHY JOHANNA JOSEPH. She
      was born on 17 Dec 1901 in New London, Connecticut, and died
      on 14 Oct 1982 in Port Angeles, Washington.
iii. (105) EDGAR MAITLAND VANCE, Sr, (page 60) was born
      on 22 May 1908 in Lexington, Kentucky, and died on 12 Jul 1979
      in Santa Monica California. He married (1) MARIE DOROTHY
      MAYO on 8 Apr 1930 in Clark, Washington. She was born on
      24 Nov 1911 in Modesto, California, and died on 21 Feb 1996 in
      Modesto, California. He married (2) VINA AVANELLE WOOL-
      LEY on 3 Sep 1942 in Salt Lake, Utah. He married (3) JESSIE L EL-
      DRIDGE in 1950 in Santa Monica, Los Angeles, California. She was
      born on 9 Mar 1906 in Robertson, Tennessee, and died on 15 Nov
      1990 in Santa Barbara, California.

50. ERNEST WORD VANCE (James Harvey[4], David Graham[3], William
     Kirkpatrick[2], Dr. Patrick[1]) was born on 22 Apr 1882 in Rome, Georgia,
     and died on 10 Mar 1951 in Eufaula, Alabama. He married LUCIA AR-
     NOLD EDWARDS on 7 Aug 1906 in Houston County, Georgia. She was
     born on 10 Mar 1886 in Perry, Georgia, and died on 24 Dec 1977 in Eu-
     faula, Alabama.

     Ernest Word Vance and Lucia Arnold Edwards had the following children:
     i.   CELESTE VANCE was born on 1 Dec 1908 in Georgia. She died
           on 1 Aug 1997 in Richmond, Virginia. She married JAMES ASHBY
           MONCURE, Jr, on 11 Oct 1930. He was born on 15 Sep 1899 in
           Richmond, Virginia, and died on 14 Jul 1989 in Richmond, Virgin-
           ia. They had one child: born in 1937 in Richmond, Virginia (mis-
           carriage).
     ii.   (106) MILDRED VANCE (page 60) was born on 14 Jun 1910 in
           Fort Valley, Georgia, and died on 21 Jan 1998 in Eufaula, Alabama.
           She married JAMES GORMAN HOUSTON, Sr on 14 Nov 1931 in
           Eufaula, Alabama. He was born on 3 Feb 1904 in Barbour County,
           Alabama, and died on 25 Oct 1954 in Eufaula, Alabama.
     iii. (107) ERNEST WORD VANCE, Jr, (page 61) was born on 31 Aug
           1915 in Alabama and died on 1 Mar 1972 in Duval, Florida. He
           married MARY KATHRYN. She was born on 19 Jan 1919 and died
           on 31 Dec 1973 in Saint Johns, Florida.

51. JOHN BOYD VANCE (James Harvey[4], David Graham[3], William Kirk-
     patrick[2], Dr. Patrick[1]) was born on 21 Dec 1886 in Georgia and died on 2
     Oct 1967 in Fort Valley, Georgia. He married OLA BEALE HARWELL.
     She was born on 14 Mar 1885 in Georgia and died on 10 May 1976 in
     Fort Valley, Georgia.

     John Boyd Vance and Ola Beale Harwell had the following child:
     i.   CAROLYN VANCE was born about 1913 in Georgia. She appears
           in the census until 1930 and is not living with her parents in 1940.

52. CLARENCE LUCIAN VANCE (Charles Nicholas[4], David Graham[3], Wil-
     liam Kirkpatrick[2], Dr. Patrick[1]) was born on 2 Jul 1886 in Georgia. He
     died on 25 Oct 1957. He married EDNA MAE ELUM on 6 May 1910 in
     Cincinnati, Ohio. She was born on 12 Mar 1892 in Ohio and died on 26
     Mar 1954 in Birmingham, Alabama.

     Clarence Lucian Vance and Edna Mae Elum had the following children:
     i.   CLARENCE JOSEPH VANCE was born on 2 Jul 1913 in Alabama
           and died on 23 Mar 2001 in Pell City, Alabama. He married MARY
           JEAN BURTON. She was born on 19 Jan 1919 in Walker County,
           Alabama, and died on 21 Jan 2007 in Springfield, Missouri.
     ii.   FREDERICK NICHOLAS VANCE was born on 11 Jun 1917 in Ala-
           bama and died on 21 Nov 1978 in Birmingham, Alabama.
     iii. HELEN LOUISA VANCE was born about 1922 in Alabama and
           married WILLIAM LEFORD SMITH of Alabama in 1941 in Ala-
           bama.
     iv.   CHARLES ROY VANCE was born on 1 Apr 1926 in Alabama and
           died on 10 Oct 2012 in Birmingham, Alabama.

53. MARY INEZ VANCE (Charles Nicholas[4], David Graham[3], William Kirk-
     patrick[2], Dr. Patrick[1]) was born on 4 Aug 1888 in Georgia. She married
     HARVEY GORDON KNOTT. He was born on 23 Oct 1890 in Georgia
     and died on 6 Mar 1936 in Lynchburg, Virginia.

Harvey Gordon Knott and Mary Inez Vance had the following child:
  i.   HARVEY G KNOTT was born about 1927 in Virginia.

54. NICHOLAS ROUSSEAU VANCE (Charles Nicholas[4], David Graham[3], William Kirkpatrick[2], Dr. Patrick[1]) was born on 10 Feb 1892 in Georgia and died on 16 Oct 1955 in Birmingham, Alabama. He married MARGARET LOUISE "SUG" DULION on 12 Aug 1923. She was born on 5 Jun 1903 in Alabama and died on 12 Dec 1976 in Birmingham, Alabama.

Nicholas Rousseau Vance and Margaret Louise Dulion had the following children:
  i.   KATHERINE DULION VANCE was born on 4 Sep 1924 in Alabama and died Aug 1992. She married CHARLES JOSEPH HEYER on 9 Jun 1947.
  ii. MARGARET ISABELLE VANCE was born on 8 Jan 1928 in Birmingham Junction, Alabama and died on 30 Aug 2004. She married SCHLOSSER.
  iii. MARY J VANCE was born about 1930 in Alabama.
  iv. NICHOLAS ROUSSEAU VANCE Jr was born about 1935 in Alabama.

55. OSCAR FRANCIS VANCE (David Francis[4], David Graham[3], William Kirkpatrick[2], Dr. Patrick[1]) was born on 18 Nov 1880 in Georgia. He died on 15 Aug 1958 in Bibb County, Georgia. He married ELIZABETH LUCY B REESE on 17 Dec 1914 in Houston County, Georgia. She was born on 6 Aug 1882 in Thomasville, Georgia, and died on 21 Sep 1968 in Macon, Georgia.

Oscar Francis Vance and Elizabeth Lucy B Reese had the following children:
  i.   JULIA E VANCE was born on 7 Nov 1918 in Georgia and died on 6 Aug 2010 in Florida. She married WALKER. There is no proof this is the correct data for Julia. She is listed in her brother's obituary in 2003 as having Walker as a last name living in Ponte Vedra, Florida. The birth and death date may not be correct.
  ii. (109) ELEANOR REESE VANCE (page 61) was born on 12 Aug 1919 in Macon, Georgia. She died on 12 Jan 1998 in Atlanta, Georgia. She married MARION SPEER HEYWARD. He was born on 17 Dec 1917 in Macon, Georgia and died on 24 Jun 2001 in Atlanta, Georgia.
  iii. (110) WILLIAM POOLE VANCE (page 62) was born on 6 Dec 1921 in Macon, Georgia and died on 4 May 2003 in Macon. He married FRANCES IRENE COONER. She was born on 5 Dec 1922 in Macon, Georgia, and died on 18 Dec 2010 in Macon.
  iv. (111) CHARLES BEAUFORT VANCE (page 62) was born on 25 Feb 1923 in Macon, Georgia, and died on 28 Jun 1998 in Bibb County, Georgia. He married JULIA JOSEPHINE LOGAN. She was born on 8 Jan 1925 in Ware Shoals, South Carolina, and died on 7 Sep 2006 in Macon, Georgia.

56. FLORENCE ELIZABETH VANCE (Henry Clay[4], David Graham[3], William Kirkpatrick[2], Dr. Patrick[1]) was born on 14 Oct 1884 in Georgia and died in Apr 1975 in Jasper, Alabama. She married CHARLES LELLARD BURTON in 1905 in Gwinnett County, Georgia. He was born on 25 Oct 1882 in Georgia and died on 15 Dec 1952 in Jasper, Alabama.

Charles Lellard Burton and Florence Elizabeth Vance had the following children:

    i.   (112) ANNIE LAURIE BURTON (page 63) was born on 17 Jan 1917 in Walker County, Alabama, and died on 11 Apr 1996 in Mobile, Alabama. She married WILLIAM HOWARD SPARKS. He was born on 11 Oct 1910 in Jasper, Alabama, and died on 15 Apr 1989 in Mobile, Alabama.

    ii.   MARY JEAN BURTON was born on 19 Jan 1919 in Walker County, Alabama, and died on 21 Jan 2007 in Springfield, Missouri. She married CLARENCE JOSEPH VANCE, son of Clarence Lucian Vance (second cousin?). He was born on 2 Jul 1913 in Alabama and died on 23 Mar 2001 in Pell City, Alabama.

57.   HENRY CLAY VANCE, Jr, (Henry Clay[4], David Graham[3], William Kirkpatrick[2], Dr. Patrick[1]) was born on 12 Dec 1890 in Orlando, Florida, and died in Dec 1963 in Alabama. He married ALICE VIRGINIA GORDON before 1912 in Birmingham, Alabama. She was born on 11 Jan 1893 in Alabama and died on 30 Dec 1973 in Birmingham, Alabama.

Henry Clay Vance Jr and Alice Virginia Gordon had the following child:

    i.   (113) FLORENCE VIRGINIA VANCE (page 63) was born on 12 Jan 1913 in Alabama. She died on 31 Jan 2000 in Birmingham, Alabama. She married EDWARD DAVID HAIGLER in Birmingham. He was born on 23 Mar 1912 in Birmingham, Alabama, and died on 18 Feb 1993 in Birmingham.

58.   JOSEPH VANCE CHAPMAN (Fannie M[4], David Graham[3], William Kirkpatrick[2], Dr. Patrick[1]) was born on 30 Jun 1888 in Georgia and died on 23 Nov 1971 in Tuscumbia, Alabama. He married ANNE SMITH KEYS on 3 Nov 1919 in Tuscumbia. She was born on 16 Aug 1899 in Tuscumbia and died on 2 Aug 1988 in Tuscumbia.

Joseph Vance Chapman and Anne Smith Keys had the following child:

    i.   JOSEPH VANCE CHAPMAN was born on 2 Aug 1920 in Alabama. He died on 4 Jun 1943 (WWII Casualty Lists, Air Corps[58]).

59.   CORA ALLINE VANCE (Edgar Walter[4], David Graham[3], William Kirkpatrick[2], Dr. Patrick[1]) was born on 24 Jun 1886 in Buford, Georgia, and died on 5 Feb 1975 in Buford. She married (1) HORACE WADLEIGH ALLEN, son of Bonaparte "Bona" Allen Sr and Louisa Jane Stanley (cousin), on 26 Apr 1904 in Buford, Georgia. He was born on 9 May 1886 in Buford, Georgia, and died on 15 Feb 1920 in Buford, Georgia. She married (2) JAMES GRIFFIN WILLIAMS, DDS, about 1921. He was born on 8 Dec 1885 in Alexandria, Louisiana and died on 9 Aug 1968 in Atlanta, Georgia.

Horace Wadleigh Allen and Cora Alline Vance had the following children:

    i.   (114) BARBARA ALLEN (page 63) was born on 20 Feb 1905 in Buford, Georgia, and died on 29 Apr 2001 in Ormond Beach, Florida. She married ROBERT THOMAS FRENCH HEADLEY. He was born about 1907.

    ii.   (115) BONAPARTE "LITTLE BONA" ALLEN III (page 63) was

---

58. "United States World War II Army Enlistment Records, 1938-1946," database, *FamilySearch* (https://familysearch.org/ark:/61903/1:1:KM61-ZRW : accessed 1 September 2015), Joseph V Jr Chapman, enlisted 12 Jul 1941, Montgomery, Alabama; citing "Electronic Army Serial Number Merged File, ca. 1938-1946," database, *The National Archives: Access to Archival Databases (AAD)* (http://aad.archives.gov : National Archives and Records Administration, 2002); NARA NAID 126323, National Archives at College Park, Maryland.

born on 26 Sep 1911 in Buford, Georgia, and died on 20 Jan 1986 in Charlotte Harbor, Florida. He married (1) ISABELLA IZZIE KNIGHT. She was born on 17 Mar 1914 in Georgia and died on 14 Jun 1962 in Gwinnett, Georgia. He married (2) EILEEN IRMA PERCIFIELD in Jun 1963 in Charlotte, Florida. She was born on 27 Jul 1920 in Indiana and died on 24 Jun 1990 in Polk County, Florida.

60. ROBERT GRAHAM VANCE (Edgar Walter[4], David Graham[3], William Kirkpatrick[2], Dr. Patrick[1]) was born on 9 Dec 1892 in Buford, Georgia, and died on 23 Jun 1959 in Gainesville, Georgia. He married MAMIE NEIL ELAM. She was born on 7 Apr 1899 in South Carolina and died on 26 Feb 1996 in Gainesville, Georgia.

Robert Graham Vance and Mamie Neil Elam had the following children:
  i. (116) HELEN ELAM VANCE (page 64) was born on 29 Sep 1921 in Buford, Georgia. She married FRANK LEROY WILSON. He was born on 29 Sep 1921 in Philadelphia, Pennsylvania, and died on 18 Jul 1989 in Athens, Georgia.
  ii. (117) AMELIA LEE VANCE (page 64) was born on 19 Aug 1926 in Buford, Georgia. She married JOSEPH EDWARD JACKSON. He was born on 17 Mar 1929 in Adel, Georgia, and died on 15 Mar 1989 in Decatur, Georgia.
  iii. (118) BOBBIE MAYNARD VANCE (page 64) was born on 31 May 1930 in Georgia. She married ROBERT THOMAS HENDERSON. He was born on 3 Mar 1928 in Savannah, Georgia, and died on 15 Nov 2014 in Savannah, Georgia.[59]

61. SAMUEL N PATTON, MD, (Keziah Robertson[4] Vance, William Nicholas[3], William Kirkpatrick[2], Dr. Patrick[1]) was born on 17 Oct 1859 in Kingsport, Tennessee. He died on 11 Jul 1923 in Kingsport, Tennessee. He married (1) ELLEN A LESLIE in Tennessee. She was born on 28 Mar 1861. She died on 5 Sep 1890 in Kingsport, Tennessee. He married (2) OCTAVIA MOORE after 1890. She was born on 16 May 1874 in Virginia and died on 7 May 1975 in Kingsport, Tennessee.

Samuel N Patton and Ellen A Leslie had the following children:
  i. (119) MARY ELLEN PATTON (page 65) was born on 3 Apr 1883 in Tennessee and died on 6 Aug 1960 in Kingsport, Tennessee. She married (1) JOSEPH H HENDERSON. He was born in Apr 1876 in Tazewell, Virginia, and died before 1919. She married (2) GILES HENDERSON. He was born on 6 Mar 1868 in Oceana, West Virginia, and died on 6 Jun 1939 in Union County, Oregon.
  ii. (120) SIDNEY EDWARD PATTON (page 65) was born on 7 Nov 1884 in Kingsport, Tennessee. He died on 10 Jul 1958 in Kingsport, Tennessee. He married DELLA PYLE. She was born on 30 Jul 1886 in Kingsport, Tennessee, and died on 15 Sep 1965 in Kingsport, Tennessee.

Samuel N Patton and Octavia Moore had the following children:
  iii. (121) LILLIAN GEORGE PATTON (page 66) was born on 4 Jan 1899 in Tennessee and died on 9 Apr 1932 in Kingsport, Tennessee. She married CHARLES ZIMMERMAN NORRIS. He was born on 25 Jan 1893 in North Carolina and died on 7 Nov 1932 in Johnson City, Tennessee.
  iv. (122) JUANITA LOUISE PATTON (page 66) was born on 21

---

59. http://www.legacy.com/obituaries/savannah/obituary.aspx?pid=173182578

Sep 1907 in Kingsport, Tennessee, and died on 16 Mar 1999 in San Diego, California. She married (1) JIM GREEN on 29 Jun 1926 in Kingsport, Tennessee. He was born on 2 Feb 1901 in Wayne County, Mississippi, and died on 23 Sep 1994 in Soso, Mississippi. She married (2) EDWARD GLENN MASON on 14 Dec 1935 in Yuma, Arizona. He was born on 13 Sep 1908 in Marietta, Ohio, and died on 18 Jul 1952 in San Diego, California.

62. HENRY EUGENE PATTON (Keziah Robertson[4] Vance, William Nicholas[3], William Kirkpatrick[2], Dr. Patrick[1]) was born on 1 Feb 1863 in Kingsport, Tennessee, and died on 17 May 1947 in Bristol, Virginia. He married (1) EMMA SHOWWALTER on 26 Oct 1884 in Tennessee. She was born in 1869 in Tennessee and died on 7 Sep 1885 in Kingsport, Tennessee. He married (2) DELORES "DOLLIE" ALTONIA CRUMLEY on 24 Aug 1886 in Tennessee. She was born on 18 Oct 1867 in Tennessee and died on 18 Aug 1953 in Bristol, Virginia.

Henry Eugene Patton and Emma Showwalter had the following child:
  i.   (124) ETHEL GRACE PATTON (page 66) was born on 23 Aug 1885 in Kingsport, Tennessee, and died on 31 Dec 1970. She married SAMUEL KYLE SMALLWOOD. He was born on 23 Nov 1878 in Kingsport, Tennessee, and died on 28 Feb 1969 in Muncie, Indiana.

Henry Eugene Patton and Delores "Dollie" Altonia Crumley had the following children:
  ii.   SIDNEY AUSTIN PATTON was born in Aug 1887 in Tennessee. He died in 1975.
  iii. RALPH EUGENE PATTON was born on 7 Feb 1890 in Kingsport, Tennessee. He died on 24 Mar 1981. He married AGNES ROBERTA HAGY on 6 Apr 1942 in Bristol, Virginia. She was born on 7 Feb 1908 in Virginia and died in 1985 in Tennessee.
  iv.   EDWARD KENNER PATTON was born on 17 Jun 1894 in Tennessee and died on 19 Jan 1970 in Bristol, Virginia. He married BLANCHE BESSIE CARRIER in 1915. She was born in Jul 1896 in Tennessee. They had one child: BABY PATTON was born on 20 Jan 1916. She died on 29 Nov 1917.
  v.   CHARLIE W PATTON was born in Oct 1898 in Tennessee. He died in 1975.

63. MARY FRANCES PATTON (Keziah Robertson[4] Vance, William Nicholas[3], William Kirkpatrick[2], Dr. Patrick[1]) was born on 16 Oct 1865 in Kingsport, Tennessee, and died on 6 Oct 1954 in New Orleans, Louisiana. She married GEORGE WILLIAM SCHULTZ. He was born in Sep 1861 in Germany and died about Feb 1943.

George William Schultz and Mary Frances Patton had the following children:
  i.   (124) WILLIAM H SCHULTZ (page 67) was born on 25 Apr 1889 in Kingsport, Tennessee. He died in Jan 1977 in New Orleans, Louisiana. He married ETHEL ALMA SMITH in Tennessee. She was born about 1894 in Louisiana and died on 1 Jun 1962 in Orleans, Louisiana.
  ii.   (125) CHARLES PATTON SCHULTZ (page 67) was born on 27 May 1892 in Tennessee, and died on 27 Sep 1962 in Houston, Texas. He married MARGARET 'MAGGIE' BELLE HINZ. She was born on 27 Jan 1887 in Choudrant, Louisiana, and died on 30 Mar

1975 in Houston, Texas.

iii. (126) FRED SCHULTZ (page 68) was born on 10 Dec 1896 in Louisiana and died in 1943. He married LYDIA LOUISE CABIRAC on 3 Jun 1919 in New Orleans, Louisiana. She was born on 21 Jul 1889 in Louisiana. She died in Nov 1979 in Metairie, Louisiana.

iv. (127) BERTHA MATHILDA SCHULTZ (page 68) was born on 15 Sep 1897 in Tennessee and died on 19 Mar 1998 in Akron, Ohio. She married STANLEY GEORGE FREDERICK WOOTTON. He was born on 19 Aug 1891 in Wallacetown, Ontario, and died on 27 Oct 1986 in Columbus, Ohio.

v. (128) VANCE ROBINSON SCHULTZ (page 68) was born on 4 Sep 1900 in Orleans, Louisiana, and died in Dec 1986 in New Orleans, Louisiana. He married MARY ALICE BAER. She was born 13 Jan 1908 in Missouri. She died Nov 1979 in New Orleans.

vi. (129) MARY "MOLLIE" FRANCES SCHULTZ (page 68) was born on 17 Nov 1903 in Louisiana and died on 8 Jun 1996 in Pensacola, Florida. She married GORDON WARREN CALLENDER. He was born on 22 Apr 1899 in New Orleans, Louisiana, and died on 16 Apr 1987 in Escambia, Florida.

64. ALBERTA "BERTIE" PATTON (Keziah Robertson[4] Vance, William Nicholas[3], William Kirkpatrick[2], Dr. Patrick[1]) was born on 27 Nov 1873 in Kingsport, Tennessee, and died on 2 May 1918 in Louisville, Kentucky. She married BENJAMIN BARKER KELLY in 1890. He was born on 3 Feb 1872 in Louisville, Kentucky, and died on 15 Dec 1942 in Louisville, Kentucky.

Benjamin Barker Kelly and Alberta Bertie Patton had the following children:

i. (130) CHARLES ROBERT KELLY (page 68) was born on 25 Aug 1896 in Louisville, Kentucky, and died on 19 Aug 1963 in Louisville. He married (1) MONICA ALCANTARA. She was born on 11 Dec 1915 in Buhi Camarines Sur Philippine Islands. She died on 29 Nov 1941 in Buhi Camarines Sur. He married (2) MARIE "MOLLIE" TSU. She was born on 25 Sep 1909 in China and died on 11 Jul 1962 in Louisville, Kentucky .

ii. (131) CLARENCE EDWARD KELLY (page 69) was born on 10 Feb 1897 in Jefferson, Kentucky. He died on 13 Oct 1986 in Louisville, Kentucky, and married EFFIE LEE PARSON on 26 Feb 1918 in Clark County, Indiana. She was born on 10 Feb 1900 in Kentucky.

iii. (132) ALBERTA KELLY (page 69) was born on 6 Jul 1900 in Kentucky. She died on 18 May 1975 in Jefferson, Kentucky. She married (1) CHARLES MINOR. She married (2) FRANK ALLEN CLIFTON on 4 Dec 1919 in Jeffersonville, Indiana. He was born on 8 Nov 1892 in Kentucky and died on 7 Jul 1963 in Louisville, Kentucky.

iv. (133) WILLIE VANCE KELLY (page 69) was born on 23 Jan 1908 in Kentucky and died on 15 Feb 1996 in Louisville, Kentucky. She married (1) WALTER A WEAVER. He was born about 1907 in Indiana. She married (2) ROGER MIDDLETON COMSTOCK on 7 Jul 1935. She married (3) DAVID S WEBB on 2 May 1937. He was born on 13 Jan 1911 in Kentucky. He died on 22 Jan 2006 in Louisville, Kentucky.

65. CHARLES VANCE PATTON (Keziah Robertson[4] Vance, William Nicholas[3], William Kirkpatrick[2], Dr. Patrick[1]) was born on 9 Sep 1876 in Ten-

nessee. He died on 6 Oct 1964 in Knoxville, Tennessee. He married (1) BONNIE BOYER. After their divorce, he married (2) AMANDA DUCK-WORTH. She was born on 4 Oct 1892 in Tennessee. She died in Jul 1977 in Tennessee.

Charles Vance Patton and Bonnie Boyer had the following child:
  i. (134) MOLLIE VANCE PATTON (page 70) was born on 22 Sep 1902 in Fall Branch, Tennessee, and died on 7 Nov 1995 in Chuckey, Tennessee. She married DANA TYLER BRIGHT. He was born on 29 May 1895 in Greenville,Tennessee and died on 8 Aug 1979 in Greenville, Tennessee.

66. NANNIE ROSE PATTON (Keziah Robertson[4] Vance, William Nicholas[3], William Kirkpatrick[2], Dr. Patrick[1]) was born on 6 Apr 1880 in Kingsport, Tennessee, and died on 24 Apr 1964 in Kingsport, Tennessee. She married BENJAMIN RICHARD CLOUD on 8 Nov 1901 in Kingsport, Tennessee. He was born on 10 Nov 1877 in Kingsport, Tennessee. He died on 20 Mar 1939 in Kingsport, Tennessee.

Benjamin Richard Cloud and Nannie Rose Patton had the following children:
  i. SAMUEL NETHERLAND CLOUD was born on 5 Aug 1902 in Tennessee and died on 10 Jul 1969 in Kingsport, Tennessee. He married IDA MAE LAROY on 9 Apr 1930. She was born in 1907 Kentucky.
  ii. KATHLEEN ROBINSON CLOUD was born on 5 Dec 1905 in Kingsport, Tennessee, and died 10 May 1911 in Kingsport, Tennessee.
  iii. GEORGE EDWARD CLOUD was born on 25 Sep 1908 in Kingsport, Tennessee, and died on 12 Mar 1991. He married BOBBIE GOBBLE. She was born on 17 Aug 1920 in Scott County, Virginia. She died on 24 Mar 1994 in Kingsport, Tennessee.
  iv. FRANCES LYNN CLOUD was born on 10 Mar 1912 in Old Kingsport, Tennessee. She died on 05 Nov 1931 in Kingsport, Sullivan, Tennessee.
  v. (135) MARY LOGAN CLOUD (page 70 was born on 27 Jan 1916 in Tennessee. She died on 9 Mar 1992. She married (1) WALTER BAUMGARNER after the 1940 census. He died in Jul 1944. She married (2) TROY COX.
  vi. (136) MARGARET CLOUD (page 70) was born on 17 Feb 1918 in Kingsport, Tennessee. She died on 24 Jan 1990 in Long Beach, California. She married GEORGE EUGENE HUGHES on 4 Oct 1940. He was born on 16 Dec 1917 in Duffield, Virginia, and died on 15 Sep 1973 in Detroit, Michigan.
  vii. BENJAMIN CLOUD was born on 25 Aug 1920 in Kingsport, Tennessee. He died on 28 Aug 1920.
  viii. (137) JANE CLOUD (page 70) was born on 9 Aug 1922 in Kingsport, Tennessee. She died on 1 Nov 1952 in Kingsport. She married JAMES CHANEY.
  ix. MADELINE CLOUD was born about 1925 in Tennessee and probably died before 1940.

67. VICTOR PATTON (Keziah Robertson[4] Vance, William Nicholas[3], William Kirkpatrick[2], Dr. Patrick[1]) was born on 13 Mar 1884 in Kingsport, Tennessee. He died on 27 Dec 1973 in Kingsport, Tennessee He married (1) REATA LORRAINE POWELL. She was born on 11 Jun 1883 in Tennessee and died on 8 Dec 1955 in Kingsport, Tennessee. He married (2) ELIZABETH HEATHERLY on 10 Apr 1959 in Tulare, California. She was

born on 20 Feb 1887 in Tennessee and died on 30 Jan 1971 in Kingsport, Tennessee.

Victor Patton and Reata Lorraine Powell had the following children:
  i.   (138) MINNIE RUTH PATTON (page 71) was born on 4 Aug 1918 in Louisville, Kentucky. She died on 26 Apr 2004 in Kingsport, Tennessee. She married GUY WOOD MEADE. He was born on 29 May 1919 in Russell, Virginia and died on 26 Sep 1978 in Kingsport, Tennessee.
  ii.   (139) WILLIAM N PATTON (page 71) was born on 25 Oct 1922 in Kingsport, Tennessee, and died on 13 Jul 2001 in Kingsport. He married MABEL STINSON KISER. She was born on 8 Apr 1921 in Lebanon, Virginia. She died on 14 Aug 2004 in Kingsport, Tennessee.

68. MARY VANCE SENEKER (Mary H Mollie[4] Vance, William Nicholas[3], William Kirkpatrick[2], Dr. Patrick[1]) was born on 20 Jul 1881 in Goodson, Virginia, and died on 27 Dec 1959 in Kansas City, Missouri. She married ERNEST LOCKE HODGE on 4 Feb 1903 in Bristol, Virginia. He was born on 6 May 1874 in Missouri and died on 25 Nov 1950.

Ernest Locke Hodge and Mary Vance Seneker had the following children:
  i.   MARY LUCILLE HODGE was born on 16 Dec 1905 in Missouri. She died in Aug 1986 in Lees Summit, Missouri.
  ii.   VANCE HODGE was born about 1912 in Missouri.

69. HUGH HILL SENEKER (Mary H Mollie[4] Vance, William Nicholas[3], William Kirkpatrick[2], Dr. Patrick[1]) was born on 11 Dec 1884 in Bristol, Virginia. He died on 16 Feb 1952 in Topeka, Kansas. He married ETHEL B GILMORE. She was born 1889 in Missouri and died 1969.

Hugh Hill Seneker and Ethel B Gilmore had the following child:
  i.   BETTY SENEKER was born on 18 Sep 1918 in Newton, Kansas. She died in Sep 1997 in Arizona. She married a PATTERSON AND a GODIN.

70. WILLIAM NICHOLAS VANCE (Samuel Netherland[4], William Nicholas[3], William Kirkpatrick[2], Dr. Patrick[1]) was born on 25 Aug 1880 in Knoxville, Tennessee. He died on 20 Dec 1939 in Knoxville, Tennessee. He married LAURA E JACKSON. She was born about 1890 in Tennessee and died 1961 in Arizona.

William Nicholas Vance and Laura E Jackson had ollowing children:
  i.   CHARLES NICHOLAS VANCE was born on 11 Feb 1917 in Knoxville, Tennessee, and died on 25 Jan 2001 in Paradise Valley, Arizona. He married MILDRED SONDRA TERRY on 25 Apr 1948 in Bristol, Virginia. She was born about 1925. They had one son, Charles Nicholas Vance, Jr, born in 1952 and presently living in Arizona.
  ii.   unnamed boy born and died 12 Apr 1915

71. DAVID ANDERSON VANCE (Samuel Netherland[4], William Nicholas[3], William Kirkpatrick[2], Dr. Patrick[1]) was born on 4 Apr 1882 in Tennessee and died on 10 Jun 1938 in Tarrant, Texas. He married BLANCHE LEE CHRISTIAN on 24 Aug 1903 in Fannin, Texas. She was born on 7 Sep 1886 in Kentucky and died on 4 Jun 1978 in Silver City, New Mexico.

David Anderson Vance and Blanche Lee Christian had the following children:

    i.   (140) DAVID COYLE VANCE (page 71) was born on 20 Dec 1904 in Fannin, Texas, and died on 26 Jul 1956 in Dallas, Texas. He married MERRY LOUISE MONTRIEF. She was born on 31 Jul 1916 in Fort Worth, Texas, and died on 9 Sep 2006.

    ii.   (141) MARGUERITE LILLIAN VANCE (page 71) was born on 16 May 1911 in Bonham, Texas. She died on 23 Mar 1996 in Silver City, New Mexico. She married HOSE HOLLEY GILL. He was born on 2 Feb 1902 in Mt. Vernon, Texas, and died on 10 Sep 1978 in Ft. Bayard, New Mexico.

    iii.   (142) JOE ZEBULON VANCE (page 72) was born on 3 Jul 1920 in Texas. He died on 27 Mar 1945 in Leyte, Philippines. He married VIRGINIA R.

    iv.   JACK ANDERSON VANCE was born on 3 Jul 1920 in Texas and died on 14 May 1978 in Ft. Worth, Texas. He married ROSALIE LEVINSON. She was born on 17 Sep 1918 in Fort Worth, Texas. She died on 27 Jan 2002 in Fort Worth, Texas.

72.   MARY NETHERLAND VANCE (Samuel Netherland[4], William Nicholas[3], William Kirkpatrick[2], Dr. Patrick[1]) was born on 4 Dec 1886 in White Sulphur Springs, Virginia, and died on 10 Dec 1944 in Knoxville, Tennessee. She married JOHN JOSEPH MANNING, Sr. He was born on 8 Nov 1869 in Tennessee. He died on 18 Nov 1939 in Knoxville, Tennessee.

John Joseph Manning, Sr, and Mary Netherland Vance had the following children:

    i.   MARY ANN MANNING was born on 27 Mar 1910 in Tennessee. She died on 1 Oct 2004 in Knoxville, Knox, Tennessee. She married WILLIAM FREDRICK LONG. He was born on 22 Apr 1894 and died on 1 Sep 1965 in Knoxville, Tennessee.

    ii.   (143) JOHN JOSEPH MANNING, Jr, (page 72) was born on 26 Oct 1913 in Tennessee. He died on 15 Mar 1987 in Cullman, Alabama. He married MARGARET MURRAY. She was born on 20 Aug 1914. She died on 6 May 1969 in Knoxville, Tennessee.

    iii.   (144) ELEANOR AGNES MANNING (page 72) was born on 14 Jan 1915 in Tennessee and died on 20 Nov 2014. She married FLOYD MARTIN.

    iv.   (145) CATHERINE VERONICA MANNING (page 72) was born on 20 Aug 1915 in Knoxville, Tennessee. She died on 26 Feb 2003 in Knoxville, Tennessee. She married HOWARD SMITH. He was born on 16 Apr 1920 in Knoxville, Tennessee and died on 22 Aug 2005 in Knoxville, Tennessee.

    v.   (146) JAMES THOMAS MANNING (page 72) was born on 23 Dec 1917 in Tennessee. He died on 1 Dec 2008 in Knoxville, Tennessee. He married MARY BUSH. She was born on 4 Nov 1918 and died on 20 Aug 2008 in Tennessee.

    vi.   ISABEL BAXTER MANNING was born on 4 Dec 1919 in Knoxville, Tennessee, and died on 16 May 1921 in Knoxville, Tennessee.

    vii. (147) FRANCIS DESALES MANNING (page 72) was born on 28 Oct 1921 in Knoxville, Tennessee, and died on 20 May 2002 in Oak Ridge, Tennessee. He married MARY ANN BULLARD.

    viii. (148) CHARLES AUGUSTINE "GUS" MANNING (page 73) was born on 8 Jul 1923 in Knoxville, Tennessee. He married MARGARET BUSSELL.

73.   LILLIAN F "LEE" VANCE (Samuel Netherland[4], William Nicholas[3], William Kirkpatrick[2], Dr. Patrick[1]) was born on 26 Jun 1888 in Wartburt,

Tennessee, and died on 17 Jul 1966 in Charleston, South Carolina. She married (1) JOHN ALOYSIOUS MILTON. He was born on 21 Jun 1887 in Chattanooga, Tennessee, and died on 3 Jul 1939 in Knoxville, Tennessee.

John Aloysious Milton and Lillian F "Lee" Vance had the following children:
  i.   JOHN ALOYSIUS MILTON, Jr, was born on 9 May 1916 in Knoxville, Tennessee, and died on 22 Jun 1980 in Knoxville.
  ii.   MARY AGNES MILTON was born about 1918 in Tennessee. She died on 6 Aug 2012 in Charleston, South Carolina.
  iii.   LEONARD D MILTON was born on 2 Jun 1920 in Knoxville, Tennessee, and died on 19 Sep 1997 in Knoxville, Tennessee.

74. SAMUEL NETHERLAND VANCE (Samuel Netherland[4], William Nicholas[3], William Kirkpatrick[2], Dr. Patrick[1]) was born on 15 Jun 1890 in Tennessee and died on 24 Mar 1937 in Knoxville, Tennessee. He married MAUD AGNES BARNITZ. She was born on 7 Jul 1892 in Tennessee and died on 4 Nov 1976 in Tennessee.

Samuel Netherland Vance and Maud Agnes Barnitz had the following children:
  i.   VICTOR FRANCIS VANCE was born on 15 Mar 1916 in Knoxville, Tennessee. He died on 16 Oct 2003 in Knoxville, Knox, Tennessee.
  ii.   JOHN GERALD VANCE was born on 25 Apr 1917 in Knoxville, Tennessee. He died on 22 Apr 1996 in Oak Ridge, Tennessee.
  iii.   (149) SAMUEL NETHERLAND VANCE II (page 73) was born on 9 Aug 1918 in Tennessee. He died on 25 Sep 1999 in Hubbard, Ohio.
  iv.   JOSEPHINE "JO" LILLIAN VANCE was born on 19 Sep 1919 in Tennessee. She died on 16 Jul 2009 in Knoxville, Tennessee.

75. FREDERICK VICTOR VANCE, Sr, (William Kirkpatrick[4], William Nicholas[3], William Kirkpatrick[2], Dr. Patrick[1]) was born on 18 Feb 1888 in Sullivan County, Tennessee, and died on 19 Dec 1976 in Bristol, Tennessee. He was born on 5 Oct 1896 in Oakland City. He married (1) MARY HELEN GRAY in 1918 in Wytheville, VA. She was born on 13 Dec 1897 in Illinois. She died on 26 Jun 1957 in Bristol, Tennessee. He married (2) YOLANDE HENDERSON. He was the mayor of Bristol, WWI veteran, deacon and elder of Central Presbyterian Church.

Frederick Victor Vance and Mary Helen Gray had the following children:
  i.   (150) GRAHAM ALEXANDER VANCE, MD, (page 73) was born on 16 Jul 1919 in Bristol, Virginia. He died on 28 May 2015 in West Plains, Missouri. He married MARTHA MILLER. She was born on 13 Sep 1922 in Beirut, Tennessee and died 30 Dec 2005 in West Plains, Missouri.
  ii.   (151) FREDERICK VICTOR VANCE, Jr, (page 74) was born on 30 Jun 1921 in Tennessee and died on 7 Jun 2005 in Bristol, Tennessee. He married ANN LYTTELTON WADDELL on 5 Oct 1946 in Charlottesville, Virginia. She was born on 28 Jul 1925 in Charlottesville, Virginia. She died on 17 Aug 2011 in Bristol, Tennessee.
  iii.   (152) ALLEN IRVING VANCE (page 74) was born on 10 Jan 1931 in Bristol, Tennessee. He married RETTA JENKS. She was born on 19 Jun 1933.

76. DOUGLAS DORIOT VANCE, MD, (William Kirkpatrick[4], William

Nicholas[3], William Kirkpatrick[2], Dr. Patrick[1]) was born on 31 Jan 1896 in Tennessee and died on 4 Apr 1989 in Sullivan County, Tennessee. He married KATHERINE VIRGINIA MILLNER on 24 Sep 1930 in Norfolk, Virginia. She was born on 5 Jan 1902 in Norfolk County, Virginia and died on 30 Sep 1995 in Bristol, Virginia.

Douglas Doriot Vance, MD, and Katherine Virginia Millner had the following children:

    i.   (205) MARY KATHERINE VANCE (page 87) was born 21 Apr 1937 in Bristol, Tennessee. She married WILLIAM ROY "BILL" ENGLISH on 18 Jan 1958. They live in Bristol, Tennessee.

    ii.   (206) GENE DOUGLAS "GENIE" VANCE (page 87) was born on 7 May 1940 in Bristol, Tennessee. She married GLEN WILLIAM "BILL" KILDAY born about 1941 on 30 Jun 1962.

77.   LYNN HUNTLEY POWERS (Charlotte Lenox[4] Vance, William Nicholas[3], William Kirkpatrick[2], Dr. Patrick[1]) was born on 18 Mar 1909 in Bristol, Tennessee, and died on 21 Dec 2008 in Cleveland, Ohio. He married (1) GOLDIE B BRYAN. She was born on 18 Sep 1910 in Tennessee and died on 31 Jul 1987 in Ohio. He married (2) MAUDE ELIZABETH BRICKER on 20 May 1989 in Bristol, Virginia.

Lynn Huntley Powers and Goldie B Bryan had the following children:

    i.   ROBERT LYNN POWERS was born in 1942 and died on 16 Sep 1961 in Cleveland, Ohio, .

    ii.   JUDITH B POWERS was born on 3 Mar 1947. She died on 11 Apr 2009.

78.   VANCE CRAIGMILES OSMONT, Sr (Augusta C[4] Craigmiles, Caroline Florence[3] Vance, William Kirkpatrick [2], Dr. Patrick[1]) was born on 3 May 1874 in Cleveland, Tennessee, and died on 8 Feb 1943 in Piedmont, California. He married MARY PIERCE HALL on 2 Apr 1908 in Alameda, California. She was born on 29 Jun 1876 in San Francisco, California, and died on 23 May 1960 in California.

Vance Craigmiles Osmont and Mary Pierce Hall had the following children:

    i.   (153) VANCE CRAIGMILES OSMONT, Jr, (page 74) was born on 5 Dec 1911 in California and died on 9 Jan 1963 in Santa Clara, California. He married (1) BARBARA ELIZABETH PARKER on 7 Aug 1937. She was born on 6 Aug 1914 in Piedmont, California, and died on 7 Jan 1969 in San Diego, California. He married (2) FLORENCE ANDREWS on 28 Apr 1962 in San Mateo, California. She was born about 1915.

    ii.   (154) BETTY OSMONT (page 74) was born on 9 Sep 1914 in Piedmont, California. She died on 2 Jan 2003 in Santa Cruz, California. She married (1) GEORGE RANDOLPH SPARKS on 27 Aug 1938 in Reno, Nevada. He was born on 16 Jun 1911 in Lindsay, California, and died on 8 Dec 1981 in Aptos, California. She married (2) BENTON ALEXANDER SIFFORD, Jr, on 26 Nov 1993 in Larkspur, California. He was born on 22 Dec 1914 in Portland, Oregon, and died on 12 May 2003 in Larkspur, California.

79.   ADELIA R OSMENT (Augusta C[4] Craigmiles, Caroline Florence[3] Vance, William Kirkpatrick [2], Dr. Patrick[1]) was born on 26 Oct 1876 in Tennessee and died on 20 Feb 1971 in Alameda, California. She married JAMES CLARENCE SPERRY. He was born on 18 Sep 1874 in California and died on 20 Nov 1942 in Alameda County, California.

James Clarence Sperry and Adelia R Osment had the following child:

i.   (155) JAMES OSMENT SPERRY (page 75) was born on 22 Apr 1906 in Alameda, California. He died on 9 Apr 1994 in Berkeley, California. He married MURIEL A GLASS on 23 Jul 1932 in Alameda, California. She was born on 23 Aug 1911 in Alameda, California. She died on 31 Jul 1993 in Contra Costa.

80.   OLIVER PERRY HERNDON (James Vance[4] Herndon, Keziah P[3], William Kirkpatrick [2], Dr. Patrick[1]) was born on 12 Apr 1876 in Greenville, Texas. He died on 16 Jan 1945 in Dallas, Texas. He married LULA GRAHAM on 2 Apr 1900 in Greenville, Texas. She was born on 6 Apr 1880 in Missouri. She died on 26 Feb 1977 in Plano, Texas.

Oliver Perry Herndon and Lula Graham had the following children:

i.   (156) EARNEST FRANKLIN HERNDON, Sr, (page 75) was born on 17 Sep 1891 in Texas and died on 4 Mar 1954 in Dallas, Texas. He married MAMIE LORRINE EDWARDS. She was born on 27 Aug 1894 in Texas and died on 20 Nov 1981 in Farmers Branch, Texas.

ii.   HESTER LENA HERNDON was born on 23 Oct 1903 in Texas. She died on 24 Oct 1972 in Dallas, Texas.

iii. GRAHAM HERNDON was born on 27 May 1905 in Texas. He died on 26 Jul 1981 in Wichita Falls, Texas.

iv.   ELLA HERNDON was born on 4 Aug 1909 in Greenville, Texas. She died on 15 Oct 1967 in Dallas, Texas.

v.   BETTY L HERNDON was born on 19 Aug 1912 in Texas. She died on 02 Mar 1989 in Texas. She married COFFEY.

vi.   OLIVER KNOX HERNDON was born on 5 May 1914 in Texas and died on 29 Apr 1985 in Dallas, Texas. He married GERALINE KIRBY. She was born on 12 Dec 1921 in Texas. She died on 29 Nov 2007 in Kansas City, Kansas.

81.   LENA H HERNDON (James Vance[4] Herndon, Keziah P[3], William Kirkpatrick [2], Dr. Patrick[1]) was born on 23 Dec 1880 in Sherman, Grayson, Texas, and died on 23 Dec 1978 in Greenville, Texas. She married JOHN BEAUCHAMP on 27 Jun 1900 in Hunt, Texas. He was born on 30 Apr 1875 in Dallas, Texas, and died on 29 Oct 1927 in Sherman, Texas.

John Beauchamp and Lena H Herndon had the following children:

i.   AUGUSTA BEAUCHAMP was born on 15 Jul 1905 in Texas and died on 21 Feb 1998 in Fort Worth, Texas.

ii.   JOHN HERNDON BEAUCHAMP was born on 5 Sep 1911 in Greenville, Texas, and died on 23 Nov 1992 in Fort Worth, Texas, .

iii. JAMES VANCE BEAUCHAMP was born ON 28 Jun 1914 in Greenville, Texas, and died 17 Jun 1995.

iv.   (157) ELENA BEAUCHAMP (page 75) was born on 4 Aug 1919 in Greenville, Texas, and died on 9 Apr 2009 in Fort Worth, Texas. She married JACK THEO CLARK, MD. He was born on 15 Sep 1915 in Texas and died on 5 Feb 1987 in Texas.

82.   MILDRED HERNDON (Benjamin Franklin[4] Herndon, Keziah P[3], William Kirkpatrick [2], Dr. Patrick[1]) was born on 21 Mar 1883 in McLennan County, Texas, and died on 19 May 1913 in Waco, Texas. She married CHARLES JAMES MCKINLEY about 1904 in Texas. He was born on 5 Aug 1877 in Limestone County, Texas, and died on 01 Jun 1960 in Trinidad, Colorado.

Charles James McKinley and Mildred Herndon had the following children:

    i.   (158) BESSIE ANN MCKINLEY (page 76) was born on 21 Nov 1905 in Texas. She died on 28 Nov 1992 in Los Angeles. She married HARLEY PEARL WAGGONER. He was born on 19 Sep 1904 in Oklahoma and died on 3 Feb 1992 in Los Angeles, California.

    ii.   ROSS WESLEY MCKINLEY was born on 27 Apr 1909 in Texas and died on 3 Dec 1996 in Ft Worth, Texas. He married RUTH ELLEN HANCOCK on 15 Dec 1990 in Texas. She was born on 1 Oct 1915. She died on 3 Feb 1999 in Fort Worth, Texas.

83.   WILLIAM B ANDERSON (Florence Caroline[4] Herndon, Keziah P[3] Vance, William Kirkpatrick[2] Vance, Dr. Patrick[1]) was born on 20 Mar 1862 in Kentucky and died on 2 Dec 1920 in Fayette, Kentucky. (A revenue agent murdered. His killer was never found.). He married AMANDA "MANNIE" CHINN in 1888 in Lexington, Kentucky. She was born in Jul 1870 in Kentucky and died on 15 Nov 1939 in Lexington, Kentucky.

William B Anderson and Amanda "Mannie" Chinn had the following children:

    i.   CLAUDE WILLIAM ANDERSON was born on 4 Jan 1890 in Barbourville, Kentucky, and died on 28 Nov 1960 in Inglewood, California. He married JESSIE ANN TRATHEN. She was born on 10 Aug 1889 in Calstock, Cornwall, England, and died on 6 Aug 1963 in Inglewood, California. They had one son, BRADLEY CHARLES ANDERSON born on 29 May 1916 in Los Angeles, California. He died on 11 May 1936 in Los Angeles, California.

    ii.   LEILA W ANDERSON was born on 15 Nov 1898 in Kentucky. She died on 11 Aug 1943 in Lexington, Kentucky. She married BERTRAM SCHEFFEL.

    iii.   LILLIAN DIXIE ANDERSON was born on 15 Nov 1898 in Kentucky. She died on 18 Jul 1921.

84.   FINLEY BOYD ANDERSON (Florence "Flora" Caroline[4] Herndon, Keziah P[3], William Kirkpatrick[2], Dr. Patrick[1]) was born on 16 Jan 1875 in Barbourville, Kentucky, and died on 30 Jun 1949 in Conway, Arkansas. He married FLO VIVIAN LEEK. She was born on 17 Apr 1884 in Missouri and died on 11 Aug 1969 in Orange City, California.

Finley Boyd Anderson and Flo Vivian Leek had the following children:

    i.   (159) BYRON OSBORN ANDERSON (page 76) was born on 29 Aug 1902 in Oklahoma City, Oklahoma, and died on 19 Nov 1989 in Fort Worth, Texas. He married ALLIE JEWEL OSBORN on 30 Sep 1933 in Faulkner County, Arkansas. She was born on 20 Feb 15 in Conway, Arkansas. She died in Apr 1975 in Conway.

    ii.   JESSIE LLOYD ANDERSON was born on 18 Jun 1905 in Oklahoma and died on 2 Oct 1987 in Montebello, California. He married LURA BESS NAILS on 5 Dec 1937 in New Baltimore, Michigan. She was born about 1915 in Missouri.

85.   VICTOR VANCE ANDERSON, MD, (Florence "Flora" Caroline[4] Herndon, Keziah P[3], William Kirkpatrick[2], Dr. Patrick[1]) was born on 26 Dec 1878 in Kentucky and died in 1960 in Hyde Park, New York. He married (1) MARGARET C before 1906. She was born on 12 Jul 1896 in Ohio and died in Aug 1984 in Staatsburg, New York, . He married (2) CLARA B SMITH in 1906. She was born about 1880 in Louisiana. She died in Massachusetts. He was a psychiatrist who founded the Anderson School in Hyde Park, New York, in 1924.

"In 1923, psychiatrist Dr. Victor V. Anderson purchased the Mansewood country estate, where Anderson Center for Autism still exists and thrives today. One year later, Dr. Anderson founded the Anderson School. He believed that children with special needs would benefit from an integrated program that comprehensively addressed their educational, emotional and social needs during a time when many special needs children were institutionalized. He began with one student. More than 90 years later, Anderson Center for Autism continues Dr. Anderson's work; currently serving more than 200 children and adults with a primary diagnosis of autism."[60]

Victor Vance Anderson and Clara B Smith had the following child:

    i.   PAULINE HERNDON ANDERSON was born on 6 Feb 1913 in Boston, Massachusetts. She died on 11 Jun 2004 in Poughkeepsie, New York. She married LEWIS HOMER GAGE in 1940. He was born on 16 Sep 1910 in New York and died in 1964 in New York.

86.   MARY HERNDON (Thomas Renfro[4], Keziah P[3] Vance, William Kirkpatrick[2], Dr. Patrick[1]) was born on 19 Oct 1889 in Kentucky. She died on 2 Dec 1977 in Fort Worth, Texas. She married SIDNEY RUFUS PONDER. He was born on 14 Feb 1879 in Calhoun County, Georgia, and died on 23 Jun 1953 in Fort Worth, Texas.

Sidney Rufus Ponder and Mary Herndon had the following children:

    i.   SUSANNE PONDER was born on 20 Sep 1909 in Greenville, Texas. She died on 15 Sep 1954 in Fort Worth, Texas. She married BRAY.

    ii.   SIDNEY ROBERT GARDNER was born on 16 Dec 1914 in Texarkana, Arkansas, and died on 2 Sep 2001.

    iii.   THOMAS H PONDER was born about 1918 in Texas.

    iv.   MARIFRED PONDER was born on 6 Jun 1927 in Fort Worth, Texas. She died on 6 Feb 1975 in Fort Worth, Texas. She married MCGUIRE.

87.   IRENE THORNTON (Patrick Henry[4] Thornton, Harriet Graham[3] Vance, William Kirkpatrick [2], Dr. Patrick[1]) was born on 15 May 1888 in Hope, Arkansas, and died on 3 Jul 1953 in Houston, Texas. She married (1) SIDNEY CLAY WILKES. He was born on 7 Sep 1885 in Kosse, Texas. He died on 21 Sep 1958 in Galveston, Texas. She married (2) THEODORE L LUTHER. He was born about 1861 in Georgia.

Sidney Clay Wilkes and Irene Thornton had the following child:

    i.   (160) STANLEY ERNEST WILKES, MD, (page 76) was born on 21 Jun 1907 in Dallas, Texas, and died on 4 Aug 1986 in Dallas, Texas. He married MILDRED VIRGINIA STROHEKER. She was born on 3 Feb 1908 in Texas and died on 29 Jan 2005 in Dallas, Texas.

Generation 6

88.   WILLIAM CURRELL VANCE, Sr, (James Isaac[5], Charles Robertson[4] James Harvey[3], William Kirkpatrick[2], Dr. Patrick[1]) was born in Jul 1889 in Alexandria, Virginia, and died in 1965 in Nashville, Tennessee. He married NELLA PATTERSON. She was born in 1891 in Pennsylvania and died in 1954 in Washington, D.C.

---

60. https://www.andersoncenterforautism.org/web/guest/about-us/history

William Currell Vance and Nella Patterson had the following children:
  i.   WILLIAM CURRELL VANCE, Jr, was born in 1929. He died in
        1949 in Davidson County, Tennessee.
  ii.   JANE S VANCE was born about 1919 in Tennessee.

89. AGNES WILKIE VANCE (James Isaac[5], Charles Robertson[4] James Har-
     vey[3], William Kirkpatrick[2], Dr. Patrick[1]) was born on 4 Jul 1893 in Bristol,
     Tennessee. She died on 18 Aug 1963. She married ALLEN DOUGLAS
     BERRY. He was born on 12 May 1891 in Nashville, Tennessee. He died
     on 7 May 1960.

Allen Douglas Berry and Agnes Wilkie Vance had the following children:
  i.   (161) MARY CURRELL BERRY (page 76) was born on 1 Jul 1915
        in Nashville, Tennessee. She died on 19 Jan 2004 in Peterborough,
        New Hampshire. She married HERNDON ALBERT OLIVER. He
        was born on 3 Apr 1911 in Nashville, Tennessee, and died on 02
        Oct 1998 in Nashville, Tennessee.
  ii.   WILLIAM WELLS BERRY, Sr, was born on 10 Sep 1917 in Tennes-
        see. He died on 6 Nov 2001 in Nashville, Tennessee. He married
        MARY JOHN ATWELL in 1941. She was born on 4 Aug 1915 in
        Tennessee and died in 1986.
  iii. (162) ALLEN DOUGLAS BERRY, Jr, (page 76) was born on 6 Feb
        1923 in Nashville, Tennessee. He died on 19 Jul 2015 in Franklin,
        Tennessee. He married PATSY STAMPER. She was born in 1928
        and died in 2012.
  iv.   JAMES I VANCE BERRY was born on 25 Nov 1925 in Nashville,
        Tennessee and died on 8 Aug 2006 in Nashville, Tennessee.

90. RUTH ARMSTRONG VANCE (James Isaac[5], Charles Robertson[4] James
     Harvey[3], William Kirkpatrick[2], Dr. Patrick[1]) was born on 2 Dec 1894 in
     Norfolk, Virginia. She died on 28 Jan 1958 in Nashville, Tennessee. She
     married GEORGE WIMBERLY KILLEBREW II on 8 Apr 1920 in Virgin-
     ia. He was born on 8 Jul 1894 in Mount Pleasant, Tennessee. He died on
     9 Jul 1958 in Nashville, Tennessee.

George Wimberley Killebrew II and Ruth Armstrong Vance had the following children:
  i.   (163) GEORGE WIMBERLEY KILLEBREW III (page 77) was
        born on 20 Oct 1921 in Tennessee. He died on 19 Dec 1992 in Peb-
        ble Beach, California. He married KATHERINE LOUISE "KATY
        LOU" MARTIN on 19 Aug 1950 in Nashville, Tennessee. She was
        born on 19 Feb 1927 in Nashville and died on 4 Aug 2011 in Pebble
        Beach, California.
  ii.   JAMES VANCE KILLEBREW was born on 27 Nov 1923 in Ten-
        nessee. He died on 23 Jul 1994 in San Antonio, Texas. He married
        MARGARET TROTTER on 3 Jul 1949. She was born on 20 Jul 1924
        in Arkansas and died on 17 Jun 1979 in San Antonio, Texas.
  iii. (164) WILLIAM CURRELL KILLEBREW (page 77) was born
        on 5 Jun 1925 in Nashville, Tennessee. He died on 10 May 1987 in
        Nashville, Tennessee. He married CATHERINE KEEBLE who was
        born 8 Oct 1932 in Nashville and died on 5 Mar 2016 in Nashville.
  iv.   RUTH VANCE KILLEBREW was born on 27 Jan 1928 in Tennes-
        see. She died on 1 Jan 1987 in Travis, Texas. She married BER-
        NARD C GREGORY. He was born on 17 Sep 1924 and died on 06
        Aug 1971.
  v.   MAMIE CURRELL KILLEBREW was born on 15 Nov 1931 in Ten-
        nessee. She died on 26 Apr 2003 in Nashville, Tennessee. She mar-

ried WILLIAM SPENCER STROWD on 3 Oct 1953. He was born on 12 Nov 1926 in Tennessee and died on 11 Feb 2001 in Nashville, Tennessee.

vi.   DOVA F KILLIBREW was born about 1932 in Tennessee.

91.   CHARLES ROBERTSON VANCE, Sr, (James Isaac[5], Charles Robertson[4] James Harvey[3], William Kirkpatrick[2], Dr. Patrick[1]) was born on 27 Nov 1899 in Nashville, Tennessee. He died on 4 Jan 1963 in Greensboro, North Carolina. He married MAURINE MOORE on 24 Feb 1925 She was born 18 May 1902 in Guilford County, North Carolina,and died on 1 Aug 1987 in Greensboro, North Carolina.

Charles Robertson Vance Sr and Maurine Moore had the following children:

i.   CHARLES ROBERTSON VANCE, Jr, was born on 16 Apr 1926 in Greensboro, North Carolina. He died on 6 Oct 1994 in Smithfield, North Carolina. He married LILLIAN.

ii.   JAMES ISAAC VANCE was born on 8 Dec 1932 in Greensboro, North Carolina. He died on 27 May 1956 in Panama.

iii.   THOMAS MOORE VANCE was born on 23 Jan 1936 in Greensboro, North Carolina. He died on 22 Jan 2000 in Greensboro, North Carolina. He married KAY FRANCES SMITH about 1962 in Lincolnton, North Carolina. She was born on 18 May 1939 in Lincolnton, North Carolina, and died on 13 Mar 1988 in Jefferson County, Kentucky.

92.   MARGARET LETITIA HEDRICK (Rebekah Malinda[5], Charles Robertson[4], James Harvey[3], William Kirkpatrick[2], Dr. Patrick[1]) was born on 19 May 1900 in Bristol, Tennessee. She died on 6 Dec 1983 in Bristol. She married WILLIAM WASHINGTON NICKELS, Sr, on 20 Jun 1922 in Sullivan, Tennessee. He was born on 2 May 1900 and died on 19 Sep 1961 in Bristol, Tennessee.

William Washington Nickels and Margaret Letitia Hedrick had the following children:

i.   WILLIAM WASHINGTON NICKELS, Jr, was born on 8 May 1924 in Bristol, Tennessee. He died on 1 Feb 2001 in Waterford, Virginia. He married SHIRLEY BECKER on 6 Aug 1949 in Battle Creek, Michigan. She was born about 1927 in Battle Creek, Michigan.

ii.   (165) PEGGY MAE NICKELS (page 78) was born on 11 Jun 1926 in Bristol, Tennessee, and died on 27 Jun 2012 in Winston-Salem, North Carolina. She married WILLIAM GUY YARBRO.

iii.   CHARLES HEDRICK NICKELS was born on 14 Jun 1929 in Bristol, Tennessee. He died on 12 May 1995 in Blountville, Tennessee.

93.   WILLIAM JAMES STONE (Ida Belle[5] Vance, William[4], James Harvey[3], William Kirkpatrick[2], Dr. Patrick[1]) was born about 1904 in Bristol, Tennessee. He died about 1960 in Bristol, Tennessee. He married MARGARET "PEGGY" CHILDRESS on 4 Aug 1928 in Monroe, Tennessee. She was born about 1909 in Tennessee.

William James Stone and Margaret (Peggy) Childress had the following child:

i.   WILLIAM J STONE was born about 1930 in Tennessee.

94.   RILEY VANCE STONE (Ida Belle[5] Vance, William[4], James Harvey[3], William Kirkpatrick[2], Dr. Patrick[1]) was born on 25 Dec 1906 in Tennessee. He died on 22 Jul 1959 in Bristol, Tennessee. He married MARTHA AUGUSTA HORTON about 1927. She was born on 6 Dec 1907 in North

Carolina and died on 4 May 1991 in Bristol, Virginia.

Riley Vance Stone and Martha Augusta Horton had the following children:
i.   JOHN STONE was born about 1931 in Tennessee.
ii.   MIMI STONE was born about 1937 in Tennessee.

95.   IDA JANE STONE (Ida Belle[5] Vance, William[4], James Harvey[3], William Kirkpatrick[2], Dr. Patrick[1]) was born on 5 Jun 1919 in Bristol, Tennessee. She died on 5 Feb 2009 in Bristol. She married HOMER AUGUSTUS JONES, Jr, on 23 Jun 1942. He was born on 23 May 1920 in Bristol and died on 23 Jan 2011 in Bristol.

Homer Augustus Jones and Ida Jane Stone had the following children:
i.   SARA BESS JONES was born on 13 Jan 1949 in Virginia. She married JOHN CAROL KONHAUS on 23 Dec 1970 in Bristol, Virginia. He was born on 7 Mar 1948.
ii.   IDA DIANA JONES. She married MAWHINNEY.

96.   ETHEL LOUISE VANCE (Charles Rutledge[5], Joseph Sevier[4], James Harvey[3], William Kirkpatrick[2], Dr. Patrick[1]) was born on 17 Mar 1911 in Tennessee. She died on 31 May 1996 in Harrisburg, Pennsylvania. She married W M RUSS.

W M Russ and Ethel Louise Vance had the following child:
i.   JOSEPHINE RUSS was born about 1936 in Tennessee.

97.   WILLIAM V PIERCE (Elizabeth Lyons[5] Vance, Joseph Sevier[4], James Harvey[3], William Kirkpatrick[2], Dr. Patrick[1]) was born on 27 Oct 1905 in Tennessee and died on 16 May 1981 in Kingsport, Tennessee. He married MYRTLE MCDONALD. She was born on 24 Apr 1909 in Wyoming and died on 29 Dec 1996 in Kingsport, Tennessee.

William V Pierce and Myrtle McDonald had the following children:
i.   KIRBY PIERCE.
ii.   CANDACE PIERCE.

98.   MARTIN "MR RIP" VAN WINKLE, Jr, (Rebecca[5] Vance, John McCorkle[4], David Graham[3], William Kirkpatrick[2], Dr. Patrick[1]) was born on 24 Aug 1903 in Georgia and died on 4 Jan 1998 in Pine Lake, Georgia. He married HATTILU ADAMS. She was born in 1905 in Georgia and died in 1998.

M.L. "Mr. Rip" Van Winkle Jr., 94, of 1070 Copolan Road died Sunday, Jan. 4, 1998. A native of Clarke County, he was a son of the late Martin Luther Van Winkle Sr. and Rebecca Vance and widower of Hattilu Adams Van Winkle. Mr. Van Winkle was a 1924 graduate of Young Harris and a 1927 graduate of Piedmont College. He received a master's degree in Education from Auburn University in 1931 and a master's degree in Agriculture from the University of Georgia in 1937. He worked for the UGA Agricultural Extension Service. Mr. Van Winkle was past Superintendent of Schools at Union Point and Madison, past Master of Madison Masonic Lodge and a member of the Georgia AirStream Club. He was a member of Fork Chapel United Methodist Church, Greshamville.[61]

Martin "Mr Rip" Van Winkle, Jr, and Hattilu Adams had the following

---

61. Athens Daily News, http://files.usgwarchives.net/ga/clarke/obits/athensdaily-news/1998/06jan98.txt

child:

    i.   (166) MARTIN LUTHER VANWINKLE III (page 78) was born on 22 Dec 1925 in Savannah, Georgia. He did marry and have children but his wife's name is unknown.

99. HERMES HEZZION VANCE (David Nelson[5], James Harvey[4], David Graham[3], William Kirkpatrick[2], Dr. Patrick[1]) was born on 2 Aug 1894 in Buford, Georgia, and died on 14 Jul 1950 in Los Angeles, California. He married NELL LAWRENCE. She was born on 13 Feb 1899 in Ohio and died on 23 Mar 1947 in Los Angeles County, California.

Hermes Hezzion Vance and Nell Lawrence had the following children:

    i.   (167) EILEEN FLEMING VANCE (page 79)was born on 14 Apr 1919 in Alabama and died on 8 Apr 2016 in California. She married JAMES HAIS BARRETT JOYCE, Sr, on 29 May 1942 in Los Angeles, California. He was born on 29 May 1916 in San Francisco, California and died on 3 Jan 2011 in Redondo Beach, CA.

    ii.   AUDRIE L VANCE was born about 1921 in Alabama.

100. ROY HENDRIX VANCE (Charles H[5], James Harvey[4], David Graham[3], William Kirkpatrick[2], Dr. Patrick[1]) was born on 2 Sep 1889 in Georgia. He died on 31 Jan 1973 in Buford, Georgia. He married ANDY ELIZABETH COBB on 16 Nov 1914 in Milton, Georgia. She was born on 6 Nov 1897 in Old Milton - Cherokee, Georgia, and died on 11 Jan 1955 in Cherokee County, Georgia.

Roy Hendrix Vance and Andy Elizabeth Cobb had the following children:

    i.   JAMES WILLIAM VANCE was born on 25 Jun 1917 in Atlanta, Georgia, and died on 3 Oct 2002 in Daytona Beach, Florida.

    ii.   ELECTA LORETTA VANCE was born on 6 Feb 1928 in Atlanta, Georgia.

101. LEONE VANCE (Charles H[5], James Harvey[4], David Graham[3], William Kirkpatrick[2], Dr. Patrick[1]) was born in Aug 1898 in Georgia and died on 1 Nov 1955 in Fulton County, Georgia. She married (1) ELLSWORTH CARTER SIMMONS on 14 Nov 1917 in Fulton, Georgia. He was born on 19 Oct 1896 in Arabi, Georgia. He died on 6 Sep 1977 in Volusia, Florida. She married (2) HARRY CLIFFORD LYON, MD., He was born on 14 May 1906 in Georgia. He died on 27 Dec 1980 in Roswell, Georgia.

Ellsworth Carter Simmons and Leone Vance had the following children:

    i.   (168) WILLIAM STEPHEN SIMMONS, Sr, (page 79) was born on 28 Feb 1920 in Atlanta, Georgia. He died on 22 Sep 2002 in Decatur, Georgia. He married MILDRED HOPKINS KIDD. She was born on 9 Apr 1922 in Philadelphia, Pennsylvania, and died on 17 Jan 2013 in Decatur, Georgia.

    ii.   ROBERT E SIMMONS was born about 1923 in Georgia.

102. SARA ELIZABETH VANCE (Frank Armstrong[5], James Harvey[4], David Graham[3], William Kirkpatrick[2], Dr. Patrick[1]) was born on 22 Oct 1913 in Georgia. She died on 11 Jun 2012 in Bradenton, Florida. She married GERALD LATCHAW CARNER. He was born on 28 Feb 1912 in Georgia. He died on 23 Nov 2005 in Deland, Florida.

Gerald Latchaw Carner and Sara Elizabeth Vance had the following children:

    i.   DAVID VANCE CARNER.

    ii.   FRANCIS RUTH CARNER.

    iii. LAURA JANE CARNER.

iv.   GERALD ROY CARNER.

103. ERNEST HOWARD VANCE (James Fleming[5], James Harvey 4, David Graham[3], William Kirkpatrick[2], Dr. Patrick[1]) was born on 17 Dec 1917 in Alabama. He died on 4 Apr 1962 in Dade County, Florida. He married HELEN G. She was born on 21 May 1924 and died on 21 Apr 2003.

Ernest Howard Vance and Helen G had the following children:
i.   ERNEST HOWARD VANCE was born on 19 Dec 1948 in Selma, Alabama. He died on 9 Aug 1976 in Florida.
ii.   MILTON MAXWELL VANCE was born on 18 Dec 1951 in Coral Gables, Florida. He died on 19 Dec 1976 in Dade County, Florida.

104. PHILLIP TRENHOLM VANCE (Edgar McGaughey[5], James Harvey 4, David Graham[3], William Kirkpatrick[2], Dr. Patrick[1]) was born on 16 Feb 1906 in Georgia and died on 23 Nov 1978 in Port Angeles, Washington. He married DOROTHY JOHANNA JOSEPH. She was born on 17 Dec 1901 in New London, Connecticut. She died on 14 Oct 1982 in Port Angeles, Washington.

Phillip Trenholm Vance and Dorothy Johanna Joseph had the following child:
i.   (169) PHILLIP TRENHOLM VANCE, Jr, (page 79) was born on 7 Sep 1933 in Los Angeles, California. He died on 15 Nov 1997 in Port Angeles, Washington. He married BARBARA G. LINK on 22 Mar 1963 in California. She was born about 1934.

105. EDGAR MAITLAND VANCE, Sr, (Edgar McGaughey[5], James Harvey 4, David Graham[3], William Kirkpatrick[2], Dr. Patrick[1]) was born on 22 May 1908 in Lexington, Kentucky. He died on 12 Jul 1979 in Santa Monica, California. He married (2) MARIE DOROTHY MAYO on 8 Apr 1930 in Clark, Washington. She was born on 24 Nov 1911 in Modesto, California, and died on 21 Feb 1996 in Modesto, California. He married (2) VINA AVANELLE WOOLLEY on 03 Sep 1942 in Salt Lake City, Utah. He married (3) JESSIE L ELDRIDGE in 1950 in Santa Monica, Los Angeles, California. She was born on 9 Mar 1906 in Robertson, Tennessee and died on 15 Nov 1990 in Santa Barbara, California.

Edgar Maitland Vance and Marie Dorothy Mayo had the following child:
i.   (170) EDGAR MAITLAND VANCE, Jr, (page 79) was born on 5 Jun 1932 in Vancouver, Washington. He died on 14 Jul 2015 in Bathurst, New South Wales, Australia.

Edgar Maitland Vance and Vina Avanelle Woolley had the one child, Bararbara Jean Vance, born in Salt Lake City, Utah.

106. MILDRED VANCE (Ernest Word[5], James Harvey 4, David Graham[3], William Kirkpatrick[2], Dr. Patrick[1]) was born on 14 Jun 1910 in Fort Valley, Georgia. She died on 21 Jan 1998 in Eufaula, Alabama. She married JAMES GORMAN HOUSTON, Sr, on 14 Nov 1931 in Eufaula, Alabama. He was born on 3 Feb 1904 in Barbour County, Alabama. He died on 25 Oct 1954 in Eufaula, Alabama.

Gorman Houston, Sr. had several nicknames. He was called "D-mop" by some people. This had something to do with either a wreck he had in Demopolis, AL, or a ballgame there, it is not known which. He was also called "Four Putt" because of a golf tournament he participated in in Dothan, Alabama.

Gorman attended high School at Marion Military Institute in Marion, Alabama. He graduated from Alabama Politechnical Institute (Auburn University). He was a member of Sigma Nu fraternity.

Gorman married Mildred Vance in 1931. He and Mildred lived in the Bluff City Inn, a hotel located in Eufaula that was owned by Gorman's father, James Lafayette Houston, Sr. While living there, their son Gorman, jr. was born. Mildred insisted that they move out of the hotel after their daughter Celeste was born. They moved first to Randolph Street. Then they moved to Cherry Street, where the elementary and high school were located at the time. Around 1950, they built a home on Country Club Road in Eufaula.

Gorman was killed when he was 50 at his farm in Comer, AL. While hunting, he leaned his gun on a fence and it fell over, went off, and killed him. He was living at the time of his death in Eufaula. When he failed to return from the farm in Comer, Mildred, his wife sent his brother, J.L. to the farm to check on him. J.L. found Gorman dead.[62]

James Gorman Houston and Mildred Vance had the following children:
  i.   GORMAN JAMES HOUSTON, Jr, was born on 11 Mar 1933 in Alabama.
  ii. CELESTE HOUSTON was born about 1938 in Alabama.
  iii. BETTY VANCE HOUSTON.

107. ERNEST WORD VANCE, Jr, (Ernest Word[5], James Harvey 4, David Graham[3], William Kirkpatrick[2], Dr. Patrick[1]) was born on 31 Aug 1915 in Alabama. He died on 1 Mar 1972 in Duval County, Florida. He married MARY KATHRYN. She was born on 19 Jan 1919 and died on 31 Dec 1973 in Saint Johns, Florida.

Ernest Word Vance and Mary Kathryn had the following child:
  i.   LUCIA VANCE was born in 1946 in Florida. She died in Bessemer, Alabama.

108. CHARLES ROY VANCE (Clarence Lucian[5], Charles Nicholas[4], David Graham[3], William Kirkpatrick[2], Dr. Patrick[1]) was born on 1 Apr 1926 in Alabama and died on 10 Oct 2012 in Birmingham, Alabama.

109. ELEANOR REESE VANCE (Oscar Francis[5], David Francis[4], David Graham[3], William Kirkpatrick[2], Dr. Patrick[1]) was born on 12 Aug 1919 in Macon, Georgia, and died on 12 Jan 1998 in Atlanta, Georgia. She married MARION SPEER HEYWARD. He was born on 17 Dec 1917 in Macon, Georgia. He died on 24 Jun 2001 in Atlanta, Georgia.

Marion Speer Heyward and Eleanor Reese Vance had the following children:
  i.   HELEN VANCE HEYWARD was born on 29 Jan 1947 in Macon, Georgia. She died on 24 Jul 1978 in Auburn, Georgia. She married THOMAS JERRY KILGO. He was born on 2 Jun 1941 in Cullman County, Alabama. He died on 16 May 2006 in Watkinsville, Georgia.
  ii. JOHN ALLEN HEYWARD was born on 03 Jul 1950. He died on 17 Oct 2001 in Tucker, Georgia.

---

62. Posted on ancestry.com by user HoustonJG

110. WILLIAM POOLE VANCE (Oscar Francis[5], David Francis[4], David Graham[3], William Kirkpatrick[2], Dr. Patrick[1]) was born on 6 Dec 1921 in Macon, Georgia. He died on 4 May 2003 in Macon, Georgia. He married FRANCES IRENE COONER. She was born on 5 Dec 1922 in Macon, Georgia, and died on 18 Dec 2010 in Macon.

> *MACON - William Poole Vance passed away Sunday, May 4, 2003 at his home. Services will be held Wednesday, May 7, 2003 at 10A.M. in the Chapel of Hart's Mortuary. Burial will be private. The family may be contacted at 797 Boulevard. Mr. Vance was a lifelong member of First Presbyterian Church where he served as a deacon. He was a Mason for 50 years. He served in the Army Air Corps and was a member of the only helicopter squad in World War II. Mr. Vance was retired from Robins Air Force Base where he worked in production management of the C-141. He was predeceased by his sister, Eleanor Heyward, and by his brother, Beaufort Vance. Survivors: wife, Frances Vance, and daughter, Elizabeth Ann Vance, both of Macon; sister, Julia Walker of Ponte Vedra, FL; several nieces and nephews.[63]*

William Poole Vance and Frances Irene Cooner had the following child:
    i.   ELIZABETH ANN VANCE.

111. CHARLES BEAUFORT VANCE (Oscar Francis[5], David Francis[4], David Graham[3], William Kirkpatrick[2], Dr. Patrick[1]) was born on 25 Feb 1923 in Macon, Georgia, and died on 28 Jun 1998[64] in Bibb County, Georgia. He married JULIA JOSEPHINE LOGAN. She was born on 8 Jan 1925 in Ware Shoals, South Carolina. She died on 7 Sep 2006 in Macon, Georgia.

> *Josephine Logan Vance -MACON - Josephine Logan Vance, 81, died Thursday in a local hospital. Graveside services will be held at 2P.M., Sunday in Rose Hill Cemetery with the Rev. Tom Anderson officiating. The family suggests that memorial contributions be made to the American Cancer Society, P.O. Box 4406, Macon, GA 31208. -Mrs. Vance, wife of the late Charles B. Vance, was born in Ware Shoals, SC to the late William R. and Cleo Ledford Logan. She had lived in Macon most of her life, was a homemaker and in her earlier years, was an avid golfer. Mrs. Vance was a member of First Presbyterian Church, Idle Hour Country Club and was a past president of her Garden Club. She was the sister of the late William Logan. -Survivors include her sons and daughter-in-law, Steve Vance of Macon, Chuck and Audrey Vance of Hendersonville, Tennessee and David Vance of Charleston, SC; four grandchildren, Paul Vance, Elizabeth Ballinger, Sydney Hester and Julie Stephens; four great grandchildren; three sisters, Louise Edwards of Columbus, Martha Barnett of Winder and Mary Carolyn Henneberry of Macon; several nieces and nephews. -Visit www.mem.com to express tributes. -Snow's Memorial Chapel, Cherry Street has charge of arrangements.[65]*

---

63. "Macon Telegraph, The", Georgia, GenealogyBank.com (http://genealogybank.com/doc/obituaries/obit/13D7DA0FA9911148-13D7DA0FA9911148:accessed 1 September 2015)

64. "Macon Telegraph, The", Georgia, GenealogyBank.com (http://genealogybank.com/doc/obituaries/obit/104726DD15886870-104726DD15886870:accessed 1 September 2015)

65. "Macon Telegraph, The", Georgia, GenealogyBank.com (http://genealogybank.

Charles Beaufort Vance and Julia Josephine Logan had the following children:

   i.   CHARLES BEAUFORT VANCE, Jr, born 11 Jun 1952. He married AUDREY.

   ii.   CHARLES STEVE VANCE was born 20 May 1948 and died in 2016.

   iii.   DAVID VANCE.

112. ANNIE LAURIE BURTON (Florence Elizabeth[5] Vance, Henry Clay[4], David Graham[3], William Kirkpatrick[2], Dr. Patrick[1]) was born on 17 Jan 1917 in Walker County, Alabama, and died on 11 Apr 1996 in Mobile, Alabama. She married WILLIAM HOWARD SPARKS. He was born on 11 Oct 1910 in Jasper, Alabama, and died on 15 Apr 1989 in Mobile, Alabama.

William Howard Sparks and Annie Laurie Burton had the following child:

   i.   WILLIAM HOWARD SPARKS, Jr, was born in 1935 in Jasper, Alabama. He died in 1967 in LaGrange Park, Illinois. He married BETTY FRANCES WHEELER on 30 Jul 1960 in Manassas, Virginia. She was born about 1939.

113. FLORENCE VIRGINIA VANCE (Henry Clay[5] Jr, Henry Clay[4], David Graham[3], William Kirkpatrick[2], Dr. Patrick[1]) was born on 12 Jan 1913 in Alabama and died on 31 Jan 2000 in Birmingham, Alabama. She married EDWARD DAVID HAIGLER. He was born on 23 Mar 1912 in Birmingham, Alabama, and died on 18 Feb 1993 in Birmingham.

Edward David Haigler and Florence Virginia Vance had the following children:

   i.   (171) EDWARD DAVID HAIGLER, MD, (page 80) was born on 7 Jul 1940. He married AMANDA TALMADGE. She was born on 8 Sep 1943. She died on 4 Feb 2016 in Alabama.

   ii.   HENRY VANCE HAIGLER was born about 1942 in Alabama. He died on 25 Dec 1943 in Birmingham, Alabama.

   iii.   (172) KATHLEEN GORDON HAIGLER (page 80) was born on 3 Jul 1945 in Alabama. She married (1) WATKINS. She married (2) CHARLES BRYANT MORGAN. He was born on 11 Oct 1941 in Birmingham, Alabama. He died on 1 Dec 1998 in Alabama.

114. BARBARA ALLEN (Cora Alline[5] Vance, Edgar Walter4, David Graham[3], William Kirkpatrick[2], Dr. Patrick[1]) was born on 20 Feb 1905 in Buford, Georgia. She died on 29 Apr 2001 in Ormond Beach, Florida. She married ROBERT THOMAS FRENCH HEADLEY. He was born about 1907.

Robert Thomas French Headley and Barbara Allen had the following children:

   i.   (173) ALLEN BRUNDIDGE HEADLEY (page 80) was born on 23 Mar 1929 in Rochester, New York. He died on 26 May 2008 in Pensacola, Florida. He married ANNE WIGGINS.

   ii.   TIMOTHY ROBERT HEADLEY was born on 12 Oct 1931. He may have married MARGUERITE SCHREINER.

115. BONAPARTE "LITTLE BONA" ALLEN III (Cora Alline[5] Vance, Edgar Walter[4], David Graham[3], William Kirkpatrick[2], Dr. Patrick[1]) was born on 26 Sep 1911 in Buford, Georgia, and died on 20 Jan 1986 in Charlotte Harbor, Florida. He married (1) ISABELLA IZZIE KNIGHT. She was

com/doc/obituaries/obit/1140D962025A0530-1140D962025A0530:accessed 1 September 2015)

born on 17 Mar 1914 in Georgia. She died on 14 Jun 1962 in Gwinnett County, Georgia. He married (2) EILEEN IRMA PERCIFIELD in Jun 1963 in Charlotte, Florida. She was born on 27 Jul 1920 in Indiana and died on 24 Jun 1990 in Polk County, Florida.

Bonaparte "Little Bona" Allen III and Isabella Izzie Knight had the following children:

   i.   LOUISA JANE ALLEN was born on 7 Feb 1935 in Georgia. She died on 9 Apr 1958 in Georgia.

   ii.   (174) BONA I ALLEN (page 80) was born on 5 Sep 1936 in Georgia. He married JANE KING.

116. HELEN ELAM VANCE (Robert Graham[5], Edgar Walter[4], David Graham[3], William Kirkpatrick[2], Dr. Patrick[1]) was born on 29 Sep 1921 in Buford, Georgia. She married FRANK LEROY WILSON. He was born on 29 Sep 1921 in Philadelphia, Pennsylvania, and died on 18 Jul 1989 in Athens, Georgia. Helen is still alive and living in Atlanta having just celebrated her 96th birthday during Hurricane Irma!

Frank Leroy Wilson and Helen Elam Vance had the following children:

   i.   MARIANNA WILSON was born on 1 Aug 1944 in Atlanta, Georgia. She retired from CDC after decades of service, heading a lab there.

   ii.   DELIA VANCE WILSON was born on 1 Oct 1951 in Gainesville, Georgia. She married (1) ROGER RAY RODRIGUEZ. He was born on 5 Dec 1953 in Tampa, Florida, and died 28 Oct 2017 in Blairsville, Georgia. She married (2) JAMES THOMAS "TOMMY" LUNSFORD. He was born on 31 Aug 1946 in Athens, Georgia. Delia and Roger had one child, JUSTIN RAY RODRIGUEZ, born 9 Oct 1974 in Tacoma, Washington. He has no children.

   iii. FRANK GRAHAM WILSON was born on 11 Aug 1954 in Gainesville, Georgia. He is a developer in the utilities industry. He married RISSA.

117. AMELIA LEE VANCE (Robert Graham[5], Edgar Walter[4], David Graham[3], William Kirkpatrick[2], Dr. Patrick[1]) was born on 19 Aug 1926 in Georgia. She married JOSEPH EDWARD JACKSON. He was born on 17 Mar 1929 in Adel Cook, Georgia, and died on 15 Mar 1989 in Decatur, Georgia. She also still alive and living in Georgia.

Joseph Edward Jackson and Amelia Lee Vance had the following children:

   i.   (175) LAURA LEE JACKSON (page 80) was born on 16 Sep 1952. She married JACK EDWARDS. They live in Texas.

   ii.   (176) JOSEPH EDWARD JACKSON, Jr, (page 81) was born on 2 Mar 1955 in Decatur, Georgia. He married TERI SUE GALLAND. They live in Tennessee.

   iii. (177) CHARLES VANCE JACKSON (page 81) was born on 1 Sep 1957 in Decatur, Georgia. He married SYLVIA BROWN.

118. BOBBIE MAYNARD VANCE (Robert Graham[5], Edgar Walter[4], David Graham[3], William Kirkpatrick[2], Dr. Patrick[1]) was born on 31 May 1930 in Georgia. She married ROBERT THOMAS HENDERSON. He was born on 3 Mar 1928 in Savannah, Georgia,. He died on 15 Nov 2014 in Savannah, Georgia.[66] Bobbi is still living in her home in Savannah.

Robert Thomas Henderson and Bobbie Maynard Vance had the following children:

---

66. http://www.legacy.com/obituaries/savannah/obituary.aspx?pid=173182578

i. (178) REBECCA NEIL HENDERSON (page 81) was born on 26 Feb 1957 in Savannah, Georgia. She married RICHARD GNANN. He was born in Savannah, Georgia.

ii. ROBERT VANCE HENDERSON was born on 7 Jul 1959 in Savannah, Georgia.

iii. (179) ROBERT THOMAS HENDERSON, Jr, (page 81) was born on 3 Dec 1961 in Savannah, Georgia. He married HOLLY LONG.

iv. ALLEN HUNTER HENDERSON was born on 29 Oct 1963 in Savannah, Georgia.

119. MARY ELLEN PATTON (Samuel N[5] Patton, Keziah Robertson[4] Vance, William Nicholas[3], William Kirkpatrick[2], Dr. Patrick[1]) was born on 3 Apr 1883 in Tennessee and died on 6 Aug 1960 in Kingsport, Tennessee. She married (1) JOSEPH HICKAM HENDERSON. He was born in Apr 1876 in Tazewell, Virginia, and died before 1919. She married (2) GILES HENDERSON. He was born on 6 Mar 1868 in Oceana, West Virginia, and died on 6 Jun 1939 in Union County, Oregon.

Joseph H Henderson and Mary Ellen Patton had the following children:

i. (180) LILLIAN GRACE HENDERSON (page 81) was born on 18 Sep 1907 in Scott, Virginia, and died 8 Jun 2001 in Kingsport, Tennessee. She married JOHN HAMPTON WILLIAMS. He was born on 10 Aug 1903 in Virginia and died 12 Feb 1986.

ii. JAMES P. "JIP" HENDERSON, Sr,. was born on 21 Feb 1910 in Scott County, Virginia. He died on 8 Apr 1992 in Gate City, Virginia. He married IRMA WININGER on 25 Nov 1939 in Gate, Virginia. She was born on 13 Feb 1909 and died on 5 Aug 1995 in Gate City, Virginia.

iii. (181) LORETTA MATILDA HENDERSON (page 82) was born on 4 Oct 1912 in Scott, Virginia. She married LIONEL WILLIAMS.

iv. MABEL ELIZABETH HENDERSON was born on 13 Oct 1914 in Gate City, Virginia. She died on 22 Jun 1988 in Coos County, Oregon. She married LELAND BENNETT GOULD, MD. He was born on 11 Jun 1910 in Oregon and died on 29 Sep 2006 in Coos County, Oregon.

v. (182) MARY ALICE HENDERSON (page 82) was born on 15 Apr 1917 in Gate City, Virginia. She died on 15 Mar 2012 in Oregon. She married DELOS EUGENE RICHARDSON in 1942. He was born on 6 Nov 1911 in Illinois. He died on 18 Apr 1995 in Multomah, Oregon.

Giles Henderson and Mary Ellen Patton had the following child:

vi. ROSE WINNIFRED HENDERSON was born on 24 Jul 1924 in Wallowa, Oregon, and died on 28 Feb 1930 in Wallowa, Oregon.

120. SIDNEY EDWARD PATTON (Samuel N[5] Patton, Keziah Robertson[4] Vance, William Nicholas[3], William Kirkpatrick[2], Dr. Patrick[1]) was born on 7 Nov 1884 in Kingsport, Tennessee. He died on 10 Jul 1958 in Kingsport. He married DELLA PYLE. She was born on 30 Jul 1886 in Kingsport and died on 15 Sep 1965 in Kingsport, Tennessee.

Sidney Edward Patton and Della Pyle had the following children:

i. GLADYS PATTON was born on 1 Jun 1907 in Sullivan County, Tennessee. She died on 8 Jun 1993 in Kingsport, Sullivan County, Tennessee.

ii. JOHN SAMUEL PATTON was born on 27 May 1909 in Kingsport, Tennessee. He died on 10 Sep 1964 in Kingsport, Tennessee.

iii. (183) MABEL PATTON (page 82) was born on 25 Sep 1915 in Kingsport, Tennessee, and died on 11 Jan 2011 in California. She married RALPH WILLIAM BROOME on 17 Mar 1934. He was born on 11 Jul 1911 in Blacksburg, South Carolina, and died on 1 Oct 1993 in Kingsport, Tennessee.

121. LILLIAN GEORGE PATTON (Samuel N[5] Patton, Keziah Robertson[4] Vance, William Nicholas[3], William Kirkpatrick[2], Dr. Patrick[1]) was born on 4 Jan 1899 in Tennessee. She died on 9 Apr 1932 in Kingsport, Tennessee. She married CHARLES ZIMMERMAN NORRIS. He was born on 25 Jan 1893 in North Carolina. He died on 7 Nov 1932 in Johnson City, Tennessee.

Charles Zimmerman Norris and Lillian George Patton had the following children:
i. CHARLES DOUGLAS NORRIS was born on 23 Jun 1921 in Kingsport, Tennessee. He died in Mar 1942 in World War II in the South Pacific.
ii. SAMUEL PATTON NORRIS was born on 16 Feb 1924 in Kingsport, Tennessee. He died on 19 Apr 1984 in Kingsport, Tennessee.
iii. KATHLEEN NORRIS was born on 30 Aug 1925 in Kingsport, Tennessee. She died on 27 Nov 1997 in Phoenix, Arizona. She married LESTER GLENN BARKER on 23 Jul 1947 in Yuma, Arizona. He was born on 9 Dec 1925 in Ray City, Georgia. He died on 25 Feb 1992 in Phoenix, Arizona.

122. JUANITA LOUISE PATTON (Samuel N[5] Patton, Keziah Robertson[4] Vance, William Nicholas[3], William Kirkpatrick[2], Dr. Patrick[1]) was born on 21 Sep 1907 in Kingsport, Tennessee, and died on 16 Mar 1999 in San Diego, California. She married (1) JIM GREEN on 29 Jun 1926 in Kingsport, Tennessee. He was born on 2 Feb 1901 in Wayne County, Mississippi. He died on 23 Sep 1994 in Soso, Jones Mississippi. She married (2) EDWARD GLENN MASON on 14 Dec 1935 in Yuma, Arizona. He was born on 13 Sep 1908 in Marietta, Ohio, and died on 18 Jul 1952 in San Diego, California.

Edward Glenn Mason and Juanita Louise Patton had the following children:
i. VIRGINIA LOUISE MASON was born on 14 Aug 1925 in Kingsport, Tennessee. She died on 14 Aug 1992.
ii. JAMES SAMUEL MASON was born on 13 Apr 1930 in Norfolk, Virginia. He died on 3 Oct 2001 in San Diego, California.

Jim Green and Juanita Louise Patton had the following child:
iii. GEORGE ROBERT GREEN was born on 22 Jul 1932 in Norfolk, Virginia, and died on 5 Nov 1932 in Kingsport, Tennessee.

123. ETHEL GRACE PATTON (Henry Eugene[5], Keziah Robertson[4] Vance, William Nicholas[3], William Kirkpatrick[2], Dr. Patrick[1]) was born on 23 Aug 1885 in Kingsport, Tennessee, and died on 31 Dec 1970. She married SAMUEL KYLE SMALLWOOD. He was born on 23 Nov 1878 in Kingsport, Tennessee, and died on 28 Feb 1969 in Muncie, Indiana.

Samuel Kyle Smallwood and Ethel Grace Patton had the following children:
i. (184) MARY EVELYN SMALLWOOD (page 82) was born on 6 Mar 1903 in Granville, Indiana, and died on 24 Jan 1987 in Yorktown, Indiana. She married JOHN LEWIS MATHEW. He was born on 4 Oct 1902 in Fetterman, West Virginia, and died on 29 Jul 1956 in Muncie, Indiana.

ii. CHARLENE SMALLWOOD was born on 5 Jul 1904 and died on 16 Mar 1911 in Union, Indiana.

iii. (185) GEORGIA CATHERINE SMALLWOOD (page 83) was born on 28 Jan 1908 in Muncie, Indiana, and died in Mar 1995 in Albany, Indiana. She married WILLIAM SYLVESTER CLEVENGER. He was born on 23 Aug 1905 in Matthews, Indiana. He died on 3 Nov 1991 in Albany, Indiana

iv. (186) VIOLET SMALLWOOD (page 83) was born on 28 Jan 1910 in Union, Indiana. She died on 28 Jan 1987 in Yorktown, Indiana. She married HARLEN ALBERT THOMAS. He was born on 24 Dec 1901 in Harrison, Indiana, and died on 13 Jul 1957 in Muncie, Indiana.

v. (187) DELMA SMALLWOOD (page 83) was born on 19 Mar 1912 in Delaware County, Indiana. She died on 2 Oct 1993 in Peru, Indiana. She married CARY GLENDELL REED. He was born on 7 Aug 1909 in Indiana. He died on 14 Aug 1980 in Yorktown, Indiana.

vi. (188) SAMUEL FREDOUS SMALLWOOD (page 83) was born on 24 Nov 1914 in Eaton, Indiana, and died on 20 Oct 1990 in Fort Wayne, Indiana. He married RUBY MARIE WARD. She was born on 15 Dec 1915 in Indiana. She died on 20 Jul 1983 in Muncie, Indiana.

vii. KENNETH E SMALLWOOD was born in 1918 in Granville, Indiana. He died on 27 Feb 1920 in Niles, Illinois.

viii. DONALD DWIGHT SMALLWOOD was born on 2 Oct 1921 in Niles, Indiana, and died on 5 Nov 1988 in Santa Clara, California. He married EVELYNE FLEGE on 14 Oct 1978 in Carson City, Nevada. She was born on 4 Dec 1911 and died on 19 Aug 2009.

124. WILLIAM H SCHULTZ (Mary Frances[5] Patton, Keziah Robertson[4] Vance, William Nicholas[3], William Kirkpatrick[2], Dr. Patrick[1]) was born on 25 Apr 1889 in Kingsport, Tennessee. He died in Jan 1977 in New Orleans, Louisiana. He married ETHEL ALMA SMITH in Tennessee. She was born about 1894 in Louisiana and died on 1 Jun 1962 in Louisiana.

William H. Schultz and Ethel Alma Smith had the following children:

i. WILLIAM ROBERT SCHULTZ was born on 20 Oct 1913 in Orleans, Louisiana, and died in Nov 1976.

ii. DONALD FREDERICK SCHULTZ was born on 7 Apr 1916 in New Orleans and died in Apr 1993 in New Orleans, Louisiana.

125. CHARLES PATTON SCHULTZ (Mary Frances[5] Patton, Keziah Robertson[4] Vance, William Nicholas[3], William Kirkpatrick[2], Dr. Patrick[1]) was born on 27 May 1892 in Tennessee. He died on 27 Sep 1962 in Houston, Texas. He married MARGARET "MAGGIE" BELLE HINZ. She was born on 27 Jan 1887 in Choudrant, Louisiana, and died on 30 Mar 1975 in Houston, Texas.

Charles Patton Schultz and Margaret Belle Hinz had the following children:

i. (189) KELSEY MINILIE SCHULTZ (page 84) was born on 3 Jan 1906 in Choudrant, Louisiana, and died on 31 Oct 1985 in Houston, Texas. She married VAIDEN COSBY MARTIN. He was born on 31 Mar 1895 in Water Valley, Mississippi. He died on 8 Aug 1985 in Houston, Texas.

ii. HELEN R SCHULTZ was born on 8 Jul 1918 in New Mexico. She died on 16 Jan 1989 in Stanislaus, California. She married TAYLOR.

   iii.   CHARLES E SCHULTZ was born about 1921 in New Mexico.
   iv.   WILLIE LEE SCHULTZ was born about 1924 in New Mexico.

126. FRED SCHULTZ (Mary Frances[5] Patton, Keziah Robertson[4] Vance, William Nicholas[3], William Kirkpatrick[2], Dr. Patrick[1]) was born on 10 Dec 1896 in Louisiana. He died in 1943. He married LYDIA LOUISE CABIRAC on 3 Jun 1919 in New Orleans, Louisiana. She was born on 21 Jul 1889 in Louisiana and died in Nov 1979 in Metairie, Louisiana.

Fred Schultz and Lydia Louise Cabirac had the following child:
   i.   (190) YVONNE CLAIRE SCHULTZ (page 84) was born 29 Nov 1920 in Texas and died 22 Apr 1990 in New Orleans. She married (1) JOHN "JC" CARLISLE RANDOLPH. He was born 16 Aug 1919 in New Orleans and was killed in Germany on 19 Mar 1945. He is buried in St Avold, France. She married (2) PHILIP JAKE BRADBURY in Dec 1950. He was born 29 Jul 1925 and died Jun 1982 in New Orleans.

127. BERTHA MATHILDA SCHULTZ was born on 15 Sep 1897 in Tennessee and died on 19 Mar 1998 in Akron, Ohio. She married STANLEY GEORGE FREDERICK WOOTTON. He was born on 19 Aug 1891 in Wallacetown, Ontario. He died on 27 Oct 1986 in Columbus, Franklin, Ohio.

Stanley George Frederick Wootton and Bertha Mathilda Schultz had the following children:
   i.   GERALD VANCE WOOTTON was born on 20 Jun 1921 in Louisiana. He died on 9 Jun 2009 in Fairlawn, Ohio. He married MARY FRANCES BUCKNER in 1945 in Kanawha, West Virginia. She was born on 16 Mar 1920. She died on 8 Jul 2008 in Akron, Ohio.
   ii.   ROGER WOOTTON Rev was born about 1926 in Ohio who married GLADYS M SLOCUM on 2 Sep 1950 in Franklin, Ohio.

128. VANCE ROBINSON SCHULTZ (Mary Frances[5] Patton, Keziah Robertson[4] Vance, William Nicholas[3], William Kirkpatrick[2], Dr. Patrick[1]) was born on 4 Sep 1900 in Louisiana. He died in Dec 1986 in New Orleans, Louisiana. He married MARY ALYCE BAER. She was born 13 Jan 1908 in Missouri and died Nov 1979 in New Orleans.

Vance Robinson Schultz and Mary Alyce had the following child:
   i.   VANCE LYNN SCHULTZ was born about 1937 in Louisiana. She married ALVIN BERNARD JEANFREAU on 12 Apr 1960 in New Orleans, Louisiana. He was born on 1 Apr 1936.

129. MARY "MOLLIE" FRANCES SCHULTZ (Mary Frances[5] Patton, Keziah Robertson[4] Vance, William Nicholas[3], William Kirkpatrick[2], Dr. Patrick[1]) was born on 17 Nov 1903 in Louisiana. She died on 8 Jun 1996 in Pensacola, Florida. She married GORDON WARREN CALLENDER. He was born on 22 Apr 1899 in New Orleans, Louisiana, and died on 16 Apr 1987 in Escambia, Florida.

Gordon Warren Callender and Mary "Mollie" Frances Schultz had the following child:
   i.   GEORGE W CALLENDER Jr was born about 1939 in Louisiana.

130. CHARLES ROBERT KELLY (Alberta Bertie[5] Patton, Keziah Robertson[4] Vance, William Nicholas[3], William Kirkpatrick[2], Dr. Patrick[1]) was born on 25 Aug 1896 in Louisville, Kentucky, and died on 19 Aug 1963 in Louisville, Kentucky. He married (1) MONICA ALCANTARA. She was

born on 11 Dec 1915 in Buhi Camarines Sur, Philippine Islands. She died on 29 Nov 1941 in Buhi Camarines Sur. He married MARIE "MOLLIE" TSU. She was born on 25 Sep 1909 in China and died on 11 Jul 1962 in Louisville, Kentucky.

Charles Robert Kelly and Monica Alcantara had the following children:
i. JUANITA VERGINIA KELLY was born on 5 Jun 1940 in Buhi. She died on 10 Jan 1941 in Buhi.
ii. CHARLES ROBERT KELLY Jr. Charles Robert Kelly Jr had the following child: MONICA KELLY.
iii. BEN KELLY.

131. CLARENCE EDWARD KELLY (Alberta Bertie[5] Patton, Keziah Robertson[4] Vance, William Nicholas[3], William Kirkpatrick[2], Dr. Patrick[1]) was born on 10 Feb 1897 in Kentucky, and died on 13 Oct 1986 in Louisville, Kentucky. He married EFFIE LEE PARSON on 26 Feb 1918 in Clark County, Indiana. She was born on 10 Feb 1900 in Kentucky.

Clarence Edward Kelly and Effie Lee Parson had the following children:
i. ARKELLA BERNICE KELLY was born on 26 Aug 1920 in Louisville, Kentucky. She died on 5 Feb 2002 in Hagerhill, Kentucky. She married JULIUS MALONE SIMPSON. He was born on 17 Nov 1923 in Owen, Kentucky, and died on 1 Dec 1977 in Jefferson, Kentucky. They had one child, DEBORAH SIMPSON.
ii. CLARENCE EDWARD KELLY, Jr, was born on 19 Feb 1924 in Louisville, Kentucky. He died on 12 Aug 2005 in Owenton, Kentucky. He married JOYCE WISER.
iii. BETTY JEAN KELLY was born on 12 Dec 1928 in Louisville, Kentucky. She died on 24 Mar 1964 in Louisville. She married HARLEN RICHARD YATES on 21 Jun 1947 in Indiana. He was born on 23 Aug 1926 in Louisville, Kentucky. He died on 25 Feb 2015.
iv. BENJAMIN B KELLY was born on 1 Jan 1935 in Jefferson, Kentucky.

132. ALBERTA KELLY (Alberta Bertie[5] Patton, Keziah Robertson[4] Vance, William Nicholas[3], William Kirkpatrick[2], Dr. Patrick[1]) was born on 6 Jul 1900 in Kentucky. She died on 18 May 1975 in Jefferson, Kentucky. She married (1) CHARLES MINOR. She married (2) FRANK ALLEN CLIFTON on 04 Dec 1919 in Jeffersonville, Indiana. He was born on 8 Nov 1892 in Kentucky. He died on 7 Jul 1963 in Louisville, Kentucky.

Frank Allen Clifton and Alberta Kelly had the following children:
i. (191) FRANK ROBERT CLIFTON (page 84) was born on 24 Oct 1920 in Kentucky. He died on 14 Feb 2000 in Louisville, Kentucky. He married DONNAFAE GISH.
ii. (192) ETHEL "DOLL" CLIFTON (page 84) was born about 1925 in Kentucky. She died on 24 Dec 1965 in Jefferson, Kentucky. She married (1) IKE ENSEY. She married (2) GILBERT C SHOPE.
iii. (193) DORIS V CLIFTON (page 84) was born on 14 Jan 1926 in Louisville, Kentucky. She married (1) JAMES D RENEAU. She married (2) WEBSTER BIRTLES.
iv. BILLIE WORTH CLIFTON was born on 18 Oct 1930 in Louisville, Kentucky, and he died on 16 Jul 2002 in Pelham, Alabama. He married GWYN.

133. WILLIE VANCE KELLY (Alberta Bertie[5] Patton, Keziah Robertson[4] Vance, William Nicholas[3], William Kirkpatrick[2], Dr. Patrick[1]) was born on 23 Jan 1908 in Kentucky and died on 15 Feb 1996 in Louisville, Ken-

tucky. She married (1) DAVID S WEBB. He was born on 13 Jan 1911 in Kentucky. He died on 22 Jan 2006 in Louisville, Jefferson, Kentucky. She married (3) WALTER A WEAVER. He was born about 1907 in Indiana.

Walter A Weaver and Willie Vance Kelly had the following child:

i.   (194) MARTHA BELLE WEAVER (page 85) was born on 29 Dec 1926 in Kentucky and died on 30 Jul 1970 in Jefferson County, Kentucky. She married THEODORE (TED) DEZARN. He was born on 15 May 1922. He died on 24 Sep 1975 in Jefferson, Kentucky.

134. MOLLIE PATTON (Charles Vance[5] Patton, Keziah Robertson[4] Vance, William Nicholas[3], William Kirkpatrick[2], Dr. Patrick[1]) was born on 22 Sep 1902. She died on 7 Nov 1995 in Chuckey, Tennessee. She married DANA TYLER BRIGHT. He was born on 29 May 1895 in Greenville, Tennessee. He died on 8 Aug 1979 in Greenville, Tenneessee.

Dana Tyler Bright and Mollie Patton had the following child:

i.   (195) CHARLES WILLIAM BRIGHT, Col, (page 85was born on 6 May 1921 in Greenville, Tennessee, and died on 9 May 1985 in Columbia, South Carolina. He married MARY.

135. MARY LOGAN CLOUD (Nannie Rose[5] Patton, Keziah Robertson[4] Vance, William Nicholas[3], William Kirkpatrick[2], Dr. Patrick[1]) was born on 27 Jan 1916 in Tennessee. She died on 9 Mar 1992. She married (1) WALTER BAUMGARNER. He died in Jul 1944. She married (2) TROY COX.

Walter Baumgarner and Mary Logan Cloud had the following child:

i.   (196) BENJAMIN EARL BAUMGARNER (page 85) was born on 9 Sep 1941 in Kingsport, Tennessee. He married JOAN CAMP-BELL.

136. MARGARET CLOUD (Nannie Rose[5] Patton, Keziah Robertson[4] Vance, William Nicholas[3], William Kirkpatrick[2], Dr. Patrick[1]) was born on 17 Feb 1918 in Kingsport, Tennessee. She died on 24 Jan 1990 in Long Beach, California. She married GEORGE EUGENE HUGHES on 4 Oct 1940. He was born on 16 Dec 1917 in Duffield, Virginia. He died on 15 Sep 1973 in Detroit, Michigan.

George Eugene Hughes and Margaret Cloud had the following children:

i.   RICHARD EUGENE HUGHES, MD, was born on 14 Mar 1946.
ii. ROGER HUGHES was born on 28 Jan 1948 in Michigan. He died on 14 Aug 1990.
iii. GEORGE WILLIAM HUGHES was born on 27 Nov 1955. He died on 8 Apr 1975 in Detroit, Michigan.

137. JANE CLOUD (Nannie Rose[5] Patton, Keziah Robertson[4] Vance, William Nicholas[3], William Kirkpatrick[2], Dr. Patrick[1]) was born on 9 Aug 1922 in Kingsport, Tennessee, and died on 1 Nov 1952 in Kingsport, Tennessee. She married JAMES CHANEY.

James Chaney and Jane Cloud had the following children:

i.   (197) JENNY LYNN CHANEY (page 86) was born on 14 Apr 1943. She married PHILIP ANSON RIX. He was born on 26 Oct 1942 in Toronto, Canada.
ii. (198) CAROL ROSE CHANEY (page 85) was born on 11 Sep 1948 in Kingsport, Tennessee, and died on 21 Dec 2011 in Kingsport, Tennessee. She married (1) JERRY HOARD. She married (2)

ROGER GALE FRYE born 13 May 1945 and died 23 Jun 2009 in Kingsport, Tennessee.

 iii. STEPHEN CHANEY was born in Jan 1951. He died in Jul 1997 in Colorado.

138. MINNIE RUTH PATTON (Victor[5] Patton, Keziah Robertson[4] Vance, William Nicholas[3], William Kirkpatrick[2], Dr. Patrick[1]) was born on 4 Aug 1918 in Louisville, Kentucky. She died on 26 Apr 2004 in Kingsport, Tennessee. She married GUY WOOD MEADE. He was born on 29 May 1919 in Russell, Virginia. He died on 26 Sep 1978 in Kingsport, Tennessee.

Guy Wood Meade and Minnie Ruth Patton had the following children:

 i. DAVID EDWARD MEADE was born on 8 Mar 1942. He died on 20 Apr 1951.

 ii. (199) WILLIAM THOMAS MEADE (page 85) was born on 21 Feb 1947. He married STARR STEFFNER.

 iii. JOSEPH LYNN MEADE was born on 27 Jun 1949 in Kingsport, Tennessee. He died on 25 Jan 1969 in South Vietnam.

139. WILLIAM N PATTON (Victor[5] Patton, Keziah Robertson[4] Vance, William Nicholas[3], William Kirkpatrick[2], Dr. Patrick[1]) was born on 25 Oct 1922 in Kingsport, Tennessee. He died on 13 Jul 2001 in Kingsport, Tennessee. He married MABEL STINSON KISER. She was born on 8 Apr 1921 in Lebanon, Virginia. She died on 14 Aug 2004 in Kingsport.

William N Patton and Mabel Stinson Kiser had the following children:

 i. NANCY KATHERINE PATTON was born on 9 Dec 1947 in Kingsport, Tennessee. She married KENT LEE VANZANT. He was born on 5 Jul 1947.

 ii. WILLIAM KENNETH PATTON was born on 6 May 1952 in Kingsport, Tennessee. He married BRENDA L LIVESAY.

 iii. GEORGE EDWARD PATTON was born on 27 May 1956.

140. DAVID COYLE VANCE (David Anderson[5], Samuel Netherland[4], William Nicholas[3], William Kirkpatrick[2], Dr. Patrick[1]) was born on 20 Dec 1904 in Fannin, Texas. He died on 26 Jul 1956 in Dallas, Texas. He married MERRY LOUISE MONTRIEF. She was born on 31 Jul 1916 in Fort Worth, Texas. She died on 9 Sep 2006.

David Coyle Vance and Merry Louise Montrief had the following child:

 i. DAVID PATRICK VANCE (ANDERSON) was born about 1937 in Texas.
from a letter from Marguerite Vance Gill, 1990:
"David Patrick Vance Anderson is David's son. He is an author and lives in Washington, DC....His mother divorced David when Pat was 2 yrs. old. She married a man named Anderson and she took the Vance name away from Pat so his name is David Patrick Anderson." Based on the book titles referenced in the letter he is one and the same with the person in the People article.[67]
He is a "thriller reviewer" for the Washington Post[68]

141. MARGUERITE LILLIAN VANCE (David Anderson[5], Samuel Netherland[4], William Nicholas[3], William Kirkpatrick[2], Dr. Patrick[1]) was born on 16 May 1911 in Bonham, Texas, and died on 23 Mar 1996 in Silver City, New Mexico. She married HOSE HOLLEY GILL. He was born on 2 Feb

67. http://people.com/archive/washington-fact-makes-gossipy-fiction-in-patrick-andersons-novel-the-pre sidents-mistress-vol-5-no-13/

68. https://www.washingtonpost.com/people/patrick-aderson

1902 in Mt. Vernon, Texas, and died on 10 Sep 1978 in Ft. Bayard, New Mexico

Hose Holley Gill and Marguerite Lillian Vance had the following child:
i.   LINDA GILL. She married JIM BILLINGS.

142. JOE ZEBULON VANCE (David Anderson[5], Samuel Netherland[4], William Nicholas[3], William Kirkpatrick[2], Dr. Patrick[1]) was born on 3 Jul 1920 in Texas. He died on 27 Mar 1945 in Leyte, Philippines. He married VIRGINIA R.

Joe Zebulon Vance and Virginia R had the following child:
i.   NANCY VANCE. She married MOREE.

143. JOHN JOSEPH MANNING, Jr, (Mary Netherland[5] Vance, Samuel Netherland[4], William Nicholas[3], William Kirkpatrick[2], Dr. Patrick[1]) was born on 26 Oct 1913 in Tennessee. He died on 15 Mar 1987 in Cullman, Alabama. He married MARGARET MURRAY. She was born on 20 Aug 1914 and died on 6 May 1969 in Knoxville, Tennessee.

John Joseph Manning Jr and Margaret Murray had the following children:
i.   CHARLES VANCE MANNING.
ii.   CHRIS MANNING.

144. ELEANOR AGNES MANNING (Mary Netherland[5] Vance, Samuel Netherland[4], William Nicholas[3], William Kirkpatrick[2], Dr. Patrick[1]) was born on 14 Jan 1915 in Tennessee. She died on 20 Nov 2014. She married FLOYD MARTIN.

Floyd Martin and Eleanor Agnes Manning had the following children:
i.   MARY FRANCES MARTIN.
ii.   MARTHA MARTIN.

145. CATHERINE VERONICA MANNING (Mary Netherland[5] Vance, Samuel Netherland[4], William Nicholas[3], William Kirkpatrick[2], Dr. Patrick[1]) was born on 20 Aug 1915 in Knoxville, Tennessee. She died on 26 Feb 2003 in Knoxville. She married HOWARD SMITH. He was born on 16 Apr 1920 in Knoxville, Tennessee. He died on 22 Aug 2005 in Knoxville.

Howard Smith and Catherine Veronica Manning had the following children:
i.   JACK MANNING SMITH was born on 8 Jul 1950. He married LAUREL ANN DELUDE on 24 Mar 1973 in Bradley, Tennessee. She was born on 25 Oct 1952.
ii.   MARY ANN SMITH.
iii. JANE SMITH.
iv.   HOWARD SMITH Jr.
v.   THERESA SMITH.
vi.   MARTY SMITH.

146. JAMES THOMAS MANNING (Mary Netherland[5] Vance, Samuel Netherland[4], William Nicholas[3], William Kirkpatrick[2], Dr. Patrick[1]) was born on 23 Dec 1917 in Tennessee. He died on 1 Dec 2008 in Knoxville, Tennessee. He married MARY BUSH. She was born on 4 Nov 1918. She died on 20 Aug 2008 in Tennessee.

James Thomas Manning and Mary Bush had the following children:
i.   KATHY MANNING.
ii.   MARILYN MANNING.

147. FRANCIS DESALES MANNING (Mary Netherland[5] Vance, Samuel

Netherland[4], William Nicholas[3], William Kirkpatrick[2], Dr. Patrick[1]) was born on 28 Oct 1921 in Knoxville, Tennessee. He died on 20 May 2002 in Oak Ridge, Tennessee. He married MARY ANN BULLARD.

He was born Oct. 28, 1921 in Knoxville, the son of John Joseph and Mary Vance Manning. Mr. Manning was a United States Army Air Force veteran of World War II.

He retired 25 years ago from Union Carbide Nuclear Division as captain of the Fire Department at the Oak Ridge K-25 site.

Mr. Manning was a member of St. Mary's Catholic Church, the American Legion and Lodge No. 1684 of the Benevolent and Protective Order of Elks.

His family said he enjoyed music, gardening and working in his yard and that he was an avid fan of University of Tennessee football.[69]

Francis DeSales Manning and Mary Ann Bullard had the following children:
- i. (200) MICHAEL EDWARD MANNING. (page 86) He married (1) SANDRA ANN. He married (2) KATHY.
- ii. MARY FRANCIS MANNING. She married LEE CROMWELL.

148. CHARLES AUGUSTINE "GUS" MANNING (Mary Netherland[5] Vance, Samuel Netherland[4], William Nicholas[3], William Kirkpatrick[2], Dr. Patrick[1]) was born on 8 Jul 1923 in Knoxville, Tennessee. He married MARGARET BUSSELL.

Charles Augustine "Gus" Manning and Margaret Bussell had the following child:
- i. SAMMY JOE MANNING was born about 1958. He married CHERYLE RENCE PRESSWOOD on 22 Nov 1979 in McMinn, Tennessee. She was born about 1961.

149. SAMUEL NETHERLAND VANCE II (Samuel Netherland[5], Samuel Netherland[4], William Nicholas[3], William Kirkpatrick[2], Dr. Patrick[1]) was born on 9 Aug 1918 in Tennessee and died on 25 Sep 1999 in Hubbard, Ohio.

Samuel Netherland Vance II had the following child:
- i. SAMUEL NETHERLAND VANCE III.

150. GRAHAM ALEXANDER VANCE, MD, (Frederick Victor[5],William Kirkpatrick[4], William Nicholas[3], William Kirkpatrick[2], Dr. Patrick[1]) was born on 16 Jul 1919 in Bristol, Virginia. He died on 28 May 2015 in West Plains, Virginia. He married MARTHA MILLER. She was born on 13 Sep 1922 in Beirut, Tennessee.

Graham Alexander Vance and Martha Miller had the following children:
- i. MARY MARTHA VANCE was born on 21 Dec 1949.
- ii. JANE MARIE VANCE was born on 16 Aug 1951.
- iii. PATRICIA ALLEN VANCE was born on 24 Feb 1955. She married GEORGE JAMES BLOOR on 26 Dec 1978 in Howell, Missouri. He was born on 3 Dec 1955.
- iv. GRAHAM A VANCE was born on 24 Feb 1955. He married MELINDA DRACO. She was born on 8 Sep 1954.
- v. CAROL ELIZABETH VANCE was born on 30 Dec 1958.

---

69. https://www.findagrave.com/cgi-bin/fg.cgi?page=gr&GRid=44551058

vi.   DOROTHY LOUISE VANCE was born on 8 Dec 1961.

151. FREDERICK VICTOR VANCE, Jr (Frederick Victor[5],William Kirkpatrick[4], William Nicholas[3], William Kirkpatrick[2], Dr. Patrick[1]) was born on 30 Jun 1921 in Tennessee. He died on 7 Jun 2005 in Bristol, Tennessee. He married ANN LYTTELTON WADDELL on 5 Oct 1946 in Charlottesville, Virginia. She was born on 28 Jul 1925 in Charlottesville, Virginia, . She died on 17 Aug 2011 in Bristol, Tennessee. Her father was the Chairman of the Department of Pediatrics at the University of Virginia - a well-known name here in Charlottesville. I continue to stand amazed at the connectivity of all of this as I have lived in Charlottesville for the past nine years (Delia).

Frederick Victor Vance Jr. and Ann Lyttelton Waddell had the following children:
i.   WILLIAM GORDON VANCE was born on 8 Jul 1950 in Albemarle County, Virginia. He married PATRICIA LORENE BANKS on 19 Aug 1972 in Fairfax, Virginia. She was born on 3 Mar 1952.
ii.   GRAY WADDELL VANCE was born on 25 Apr 1953 in Tennessee.
iii. LAUREN LYTTELTON VANCE was born on 9 Jul 1956 in Tennessee. She married EDWARD WALLACE WOLCOTT, Jr, on 10 Sep 1983 in Bristol, Virginia. He was born on 9 Aug 1953 in Norfolk, Virginia.

152. ALLEN IRVING VANCE (Frederick Victor[5],William Kirkpatrick[4], William Nicholas[3], William Kirkpatrick[2], Dr. Patrick[1]) was born on 10 Jan 1931 in Bristol, Tennessee. He married RETTA JELKS. She was born on 19 Jun 1933.

Allen Irving Vance and Retta Jenks had the following children:
i.   JULIA DORIOT VANCE was born on 3 Dec 1958. She married WILLIAM EDGAR BROWN on 1 Jul 1989 in Bristol, Virginia.
ii.   RETTA JELKS VANCE was born on 12 Jun 1961.
iii. HELEN ELIZABETH VANCE was born on 24 Oct 1962.

153. VANCE CRAIGMILES OSMONT, Jr, (Vance Craigmiles[5], Augusta C[4] Craigmiles, Caroline Florence[3] Vance, William Kirkpatrick[2], Dr. Patrick[1]) was born on 5 Dec 1911 in California. He died on 9 Jan 1963 in Santa Clara, California. He married (1) BARBARA ELIZABETH PARKER. She was born on 6 Aug 1914 in Piedmont, California. She died on 7 Jan 1969 in San Diego, California. He married (2) FLORENCE ANDREWS on 28 Apr 1962 in San Mateo, California. She was born about 1915.

Vance Craigmiles Osmont and Barbara Elizabeth Parker had the following child:
i.   VANCE CRAIGMILES OSMONT III was born on 28 Dec 1948. He died on 8 Jan 1949 in Monterey.

154. BETTY OSMONT (Vance Craigmiles[5], Augusta C[4] Craigmiles, Caroline Florence[3] Vance, William Kirkpatrick[2], Dr. Patrick[1]) was born on 9 Sep 1914 in Piedmont, California. She died on 2 Jan 2003 in Santa Cruz, California. She married (1) BENTON ALEXANDER SIFFORD, Jr, on 26 Nov 1993 in Larkspur, California He was born on 22 Dec 1914 in Portland, Multomah, Oregon, and died on 12 May 2003 in Larkspur, California. She married (2) GEORGE RANDOLPH SPARKS on 27 Aug 1938 in Reno, Washoe, Nevada. He was born on 16 Jun 1911 in Lindsay, California. He died on 8 Dec 1981 in Aptos, California.

George Randolph Sparks and Betty Osmont had the following child:
- i.   CAROLYN BETTY SPARKS was born about 1940 in California.

155. JAMES OSMONT SPERRY (Adelia R[5] Osment, Augusta C[4] Craigmiles, Caroline Florence[3] Vance, William Kirkpatrick[2], Dr. Patrick[1]) was born on 22 Apr 1906 in Alameda, California. He died on 9 Apr 1994 in Berkeley, Alameda, California. He married MURIEL A GLASS on 23 Jul 1932 in Alameda, California. She was born on 23 Aug 1911 in Alameda, California, and died on 31 Jul 1993 in Contra Costa.

James Osmont Sperry and Muriel A Glass had the following children:
- i.   CYNTHIA SPERRY was born on 29 May 1934 in Alameda, California.
- ii.   JAMES WOOSTER SPERRY was born on 9 Apr 1937 in Alameda, California. He died on 20 Dec 2009 in Moraga, California. He married MARY P MADDEN on 5 Aug 1972 in Solano, California. She was born about 1944.
- iii.   ROBERT BRUCE SPERRY was born on 27 Dec 1939 in Yolo, California. He died on 4 Sep 2002 in Yuba City, California.

156. EARNEST FRANKLIN HERNDON, Sr, (Oliver Perry[5], James Vance[4] Herndon, Keziah P[3] Vance, William Kirkpatrick[2], Dr. Patrick[1]) was born on 17 Sep 1891 in Texas. He died on 4 Mar 1954 in Dallas, Texas. He married MAMIE LORRINE EDWARDS. She was born on 27 Aug 1894 in Texas and died on 20 Nov 1981 in Farmers Branch, Texas.

Earnest Franklin Herndon and Mamie Lorrine Edwards had the following children:
- i.   (201) GRACE HERNDON (page 86) was born on 4 Aug 1912 in Dallas, Texas. She died on 7 Mar 1993 in Kemp, Texas. She married JAMES PATRICK "JP" JOHNSON. He was born on 17 Feb 1910 in Texas and died in May 1983 in Kemp, Texas.
- ii.   HARRY HERNDON was born on 23 Dec 1915 in Texas. He died on 31 Aug 1939 in Dallas, Texas. He married LORENA. She was born about 1919 in Texas.
- iii.   (202) WILLIE MINALEE HERNDON (page 86) was born on 5 Sep 1918 in Dallas County, Texas. He died on 12 Mar 2000 in Dallas, Texas. He married BERT FRANCIS ELSEY. He was born on 19 Sep 1902 in Missouri and died on 6 Dec 1994 in Dallas, Texas.
- iv.   (203) FAYE HERNDON (page 86) was born in 1922 in Texas and died on 31 Jan 2008 in Tennessee. She married CARL ROBERT ELSEY. He was born in 1909 in Dallas,Texas. He died on 23 Jul 1960 in Dallas, Texas.
- v.   ERNEST FRANKLIN HERNDON, Jr, was born on 16 Nov 1928 in Dallas, Texas. He died on 24 Mar 1980 in Dallas, Dallas, Texas.
- vi.   (204) BILLIE GEAN HERNDON (page 87) was born on 7 Feb 1931 in Dallas, Texas. He died on 1 Nov 2013 in Durant, Oklahoma. He married ALICE FAY SHIPP.

157. ELENA BEAUCHAMP (Lena H[5] Herndon, James Vance[4] Herndon, Keziah P[3] Vance, William Kirkpatrick[2], Dr. Patrick[1]) was born on 4 Aug 1919 in Greenville, Texas, and died on 9 Apr 2009 in Fort Worth, Texas. She married JACK THEO CLARK, MD. He was born on 15 Sep 1915 in Texas. He died on 5 Feb 1987 in Texas.

Jack Theo Clark and Elena Beauchamp had the following children:
- i.   JACK THEO CLARK, Jr, was born about 1936 in Texas.
- ii.   DOROTHY GAIL CLARK was born about 1938 in Texas.

158. BESSIE ANN MCKINLEY (Mildred[5] Herndon, Benjamin Franklin[4] Herndon, Keziah P[3] Vance, William Kirkpatrick[2], Dr. Patrick[1]) was born on 21 Nov 1905 in Texas. She died on 28 Nov 1992 in Los Angeles. She married HARLEY PEARL WAGGONER. He was born on 19 Sep 1904 in Oklahoma. He died on 3 Feb 1992 in Los Angeles, California.

Harley Pearl Waggoner and Bessie Ann McKINLEY had the following child:
  i.   HARLEY WAGGONER was born about 1931 in Colorado.

159. BYRON OSBORN ANDERSON (Finley Boyd[5], Florence Caroline[4] Herndon, Keziah P[3] Vance, William Kirkpatrick[2], Dr. Patrick[1]) was born on 29 Aug 1902 in Oklahoma City, Oklahoma. He died on 19 Nov 1989 in Fort Worth, Texas. He married ALLIE JEWELL OSBORN on 30 Sep 1933 in Faulkner County, Arkansas. She was born on 20 Feb 1905 in Conway, Arkansas, and died in Apr 1975 in Conway.

Byron Osborn Anderson and Allie Jewel Osborn had the following children:
  i.   ROBERT BYRON "BOBBIE" ANDERSON was born in 1935 in Conway, Arkansas.
  ii. MARTA ANDERSON was born in 1936 in Conway, Arkansas.

160. STANLEY ERNEST WILKES, MD, (Irene[5] Thornton, Patrick Henry[4] Thornton, Harriet Graham[3] Vance, William Kirkpatrick[2], Dr. Patrick[1]) was born on 21 Jun 1907 in Dallas, Texas. He died on 4 Aug 1986 in Dallas, Texas. He married MILDRED VIRGINIA STROHEKER. She was born on 3 Feb 1908 in Texas. She died on 29 Jan 2005 in Dallas, Texas.

Stanley Ernest Wilkes and Mildred Virginia Stroheker had the following children:
  i.   DORIS JEAN WILKES was born about 1932 in Texas.
  ii. STANLEY ERNEST WILKES was born on 7 Feb 1935 in Dallas, Texas.

Generation 7

161. MARY CURRELL BERRY (Agnes Wilkie[6] Vance, James Isaac[5], Charles Robertson[4], James Harvey[3], William Kirkpatrick[2], Dr. Patrick[1]) was born on 1 Jul 1915 in Nashville, Tennessee, and died on 19 Jan 2004 in Peterborough, New Hampshire. She married HERNDON ALBERT OLIVER. He was born on 3 Apr 1911 in Nashville, Tennessee. He died on 2 Oct 1998 in Nashville, Tennessee.

Herndon Albert Oliver and Mary Currell Berry had the following children:
  i.   HERNDON ALBERT OLIVER III was born about 1939 in Pennsylvania.
  ii. DAUGHTER OLIVER. She married TEWKSBURY.

162. ALLEN DOUGLAS BERRY, Jr, (Agnes Wilkie[6] Vance, James Isaac[5], Charles Robertson[4], James Harvey[3], William Kirkpatrick[2], Dr. Patrick[1]) was born on 6 Feb 1923 in Nashville, Tennessee, and died on 19 Jul 2015 in Franklin, Tennessee. He married PATSY STAMPER. She was born in 1928 and died in 2012.

Allen Douglas Berry and Patsy Stamper had the following children:
  i.   CURRELL VANCE BERRY was born on 18 Sep 1953. He married MARGOT.
  ii. ALLEN DOUGLAS BERRY. He married DIANNE.
  iii. JAMES TROUSDALE BERRY. He married MARY BETH.

163. GEORGE WIMBERLEY KILLEBREW III (Ruth Armstrong[6] Vance, James Isaac[5], Charles Robertson[4], James Harvey[3], William Kirkpatrick[2], Dr. Patrick[1]) was born on 20 Oct 1921 in Tennessee and died on 19 Dec 1992 in Pebble Beach, California. He married KATHERINE LOUISE 'Katy Lou' MARTIN` on 19 Aug 1950 in Nashville, Tennessee. She was born on 19 Feb 1927 in Nashville, Tennessee, and died on 4 Aug 2011 in Pebble Beach, California.

> *Katherine Louise Martin Killebrew February 19, 1927 ~ August 4, 2011 PEB-BLE BEACH - Katherine Louise Martin Killebrew passed away August 4 in Pebble Beach, California. Born in Nashville, Tennessee, Katy Lou was a graduate of Peabody Demonstration School, attended Ward-Belmont and Southern Methodist University (S.M.U.) Katy Lou married George Wimberly Killebrew III on August 19, 1950 and moved to Honolulu, Hawaii in 1960 where they raised their family. She and her husband retired to Pebble Beach, CA in 1990. Katy Lou was a member of the Outrigger Canoe Club and the Beach and Tennis Club in Pebble Beach. Her love of travel took her to the far reaches of the world. Katy Lou did volunteer work for Kapiolani Hospital and Punahou School. She loved to play tennis, was a gourmet cook and, most especially, loved her family. Katy Lou is survived by her children, George Wimberly (Anne Nash) Killebrew IV of Dallas, TX and Katherine Vance Killebrew of Honolulu, HA; her grandchildren, Katherine Taylor Nordgren, Brett Douglas Bechert, Whitney Martin Bechert, Thomas Nash Killebrew, William Martin Killebrew; her great-grandchildren, Jack Vance Nordgren and Joshua Finn Nordgren and her brother, Woodson James (Clara Chester) Martin Jr. of Nashville, Tennessee. She was preceded in death by her husband, George, in 1992. Memorial services will be held later in Pebble Beach and Hawaii. In lieu of flowers, contributions may be made to Community Hospital of the Monterey Peninsula, P.O. Box HH, Monterey, CA 93942.[70]*

George Wimberley Killebrew III and Katherine Louise Martin had the following children:
- i. GEORGE WIMBERLY KILLEBREW IV.
- ii. KATHERINE VANCE KILLEBREW.

164. WILLIAM CURRELL KILLEBREW (Ruth Armstrong[6] Vance, James Isaac[5], Charles Robertson[4], James Harvey[3], William Kirkpatrick[2], Dr. Patrick[1]) was born on 5 Jun 1925 in Nashville, Tennessee, and died on 10 May 1987 in Nashville. He married CATHERINE KEEBLE. She was born on 8 Oct 1932 in Nashville and died on 5 Mar 2016 in Nashville.

William Currell Killebrew and Catherine Keeble had the following children:
- i. WILLIAM CURRELL KILLEBREW, Jr, was born on 13 Sep 1953 in Nashville, Tennessee.
- ii. MARGARET KEEBLE KILLEBREW was born on 7 Apr 1956 in Munich, Germany. She died on 5 Jun 2009 in Nashville, Tennessee.
- iii. RUTH VANCE KILLIBREW was born on 1 Aug 1957 in Savannah, Georgia, and died on 22 Jan 2014 in Fairview, Tennessee. She married HAROLD VYRL GAMBLE on 1 Aug 1981 in Robertson, Tennessee.
- iv. MADALINE BOURNE KILLEBREW was born on 6 Dec 1960 in Savannah, Georgia. She married RICHARDS.

---

70. Posted on ancestry.com by user ESHAIFER

v.   CATHERINE SIMMONS KILLEBREW. She married MADISON.

165. PEGGY MAE NICKELS (Margaret Letitia[6] Hedrick, Rebekah Malinda[5] Vance, Charles Robertson[4], James Harvey[3], William Kirkpatrick[2], Dr. Patrick[1]) was born on 11 Jun 1926 in Bristol, Tennessee. She died on 27 Jun 2012 in Winston-Salem, North Carolina. She married WILLIAM GUY YARBRO.

Peggy Mae Nickels Yarbro passed away on June 27, 2012 in Winston-Salem, North Carolina. She was born June 11, 1926 in Bristol, Tennessee to Margaret Hedrick Nickels and William Washington Nickels. Her childhood was always recalled with much delight: Camp Cherokee, travels out west and to New England with her grandmother and Aunt Mary, playing with her three brothers (it was said that she was the best athlete of them all!). After high school, she attended Randolph Macon Women's College in Lynchburg, Virginia and then graduated from the University of Tennessee in Knoxville. She married William Guy Yarbro in 1949, and they settled in Dyersburg, Tennessee where she lived for twenty years. They raised three children; she made good friends and had fond memories of her life there. When the marriage ended, Peggy moved back to Bristol and into 412 Sixth Street (now Troutdale Restaurant), which was the house in which her grandparents had lived and where her mother and beloved aunt Mary Hedrick were born. She acquired her first job (outside the home) as a caseworker for the Sullivan Count Department of Social Services. After 10 years, she retired and moved to Blountville where she lived happily for a number of years, near her brother Charlie and his wife Jane. Her last residence in Bristol was at Middlebrook and during her twenty years there she enjoyed friendships with her wonderful neighbors and loved her gorgeous views of the lake. During her retirement she indulged her passions for reading and old movies. Her final residence was at Brighton Gardens in Winston-Salem. Even though the last year saw a swift decline in her physical and mental faculties she retained the essence of her personality, gentle and good-humored with a measure of feistiness. Peggy will be missed by all who knew and loved her. Besides her parents and aunt, her brothers Bill and Charles Nickels predeceased her. She is survived by her children: Scott Yarbro of Charlotte, Mary (Bob) Roudabush of Ocklawaha, Florida, Clara Yarbro (Mark Wolfson) of Winston-Salem; grandchildren Lily and Adam Wolfson; brother George (Janet) Nickels of Timberline, Virginia, sister-in-law Jane Nickels of Bristol, sister-in-law Shirley Nickels of Waterford, Virginia, former brother-in-law Tom Yarbro of Dyersburg, Tennessee, former sister-in-law Charlotte Yarbro, and many nieces and nephews. (posted on ancestry.com by user pthomp)

William Guy Yarbro and Peggy Mae Nickels had the following children:
i.   MARY YARBRO.
ii.   SCOTT YARBRO.
iii. CLARA LOUISE YARBRO. She married MARK WOLFSON and they have two children, LILY YARBRO WOLFSON, born 23 Mar 1991 in Minnesota, and ADAM YARBRO WOLFSON, born 4 May 1993 in Minnesota.

166. MARTIN LUTHER VANWINKLE III (Martin[6] Vanwinkle, Rebecca[5] Vance, John McCorkle[4], David Graham[3], William Kirkpatrick[2], Dr. Patrick[1]) was born on 22 Dec 1925 in Savannah, Georgia. He went to Emory University in 1958 for a master's in business administration.[71] I also

---

71. http://www.e-yearbook.com/yearbooks/Emory_University_Campus_Yearbook/1958/

found where he had qualified to run for office in 2000.[72] He attended North Georgia College in 1943.[73]

Martin Luther Vanwinkle III had the following children:
  i.   MARTIN LUTHER VANWINKLE was born on 20 Nov 1945. He was living in Ohio in 2013.
  ii. MARYLU VANWINKLE. She married POLITOWSKI.

167. EILEEN FLEMING VANCE (Hermes Hezzion[6], David Nelson[5], James Harvey [4], David Graham[3], William Kirkpatrick[2], Dr. Patrick[1]) was born on 14 Apr 1919 in Alabama. She married James Hais Barrett Joyce, Sr, on 29 May 1942 in Los Angeles, California. He was born on 29 May 1916 in San Francisco, California, and died on 3 Jan 2011 in Redondo Beach, California.

James Hais Barrett Joyce and Eileen Fleming Vance had the following children:
  i.   JAMES BARRETT JOYCE, Jr, was born on 19 Dec 1942 in Los Angeles, California.
  ii. VIRGINIA EILEEN JOYCE was born on 22 May 1945 in Los Angeles, California. She married JIM DUNN.
  iii. THOMAS VANCE JOYCE was born on 23 Oct 1951 in Los Angeles, California. He had a CPA license but it expired in 1977.

168. WILLIAM STEPHEN SIMMONS Sr (Leone[6] Vance, Charles H[5], James Harvey [4], David Graham[3], William Kirkpatrick[2], Dr. Patrick[1]) was born on 28 Feb 1920 in Atlanta, Georgia. He died on 22 Sep 2002 in Decatur, Georgia. He married MILDRED HOPKINS KIDD. She was born on 9 Apr 1922 in Philadelphia, Pennsylvania. She died on 17 Jan 2013 in Decatur, Georgia.

William Stephen Simmons and Mildred Hopkins Kidd had the following children:
  i.   WILLIAM STEPHEN SIMMONS, Jr, was born about 1949 in Georgia. He married PATRICIA LOUISE MCDOWELL on 26 Nov 1983 in Indianapolis, Indiana. She was born about 1954 in Indiana.
  ii. DOUG SIMMONS. He married CONNIE.

169. PHILLIP TRENHOLM VANCE, Jr, (Phillip Trenholm[6], Edgar McGaughey[5], James Harvey [4], David Graham[3], William Kirkpatrick[2], Dr. Patrick[1]) was born on 7 Sep 1933 in Los Angeles, California. He died on 15 Nov 1997 in Port Angeles, Washington. He married BARBARA G LINK on 22 Mar 1963 in California. She was born about 1934.

Phillip Trenholm Vance and Barbara G. Link had the following child:
  i.   TRACY DIANE VANCE was born on 18 Jan 1958 in California. She died on 25 Aug 1991. She married MICHAEL RAY PEAK. He was born on 29 Apr 1951 in Little Rock, Arkansas. He died on 26 Nov 2007 in Sacramento, California.

170. EDGAR MAITLAND VANCE, Jr, (Edgar Maitland[6], Edgar McGaughey[5], James Harvey[4], David Graham[3], William Kirkpatrick[2], Dr. Patrick[1]) was born on 5 Jun 1932 in Vancouver, Washington. He died on 14 Jul 2015 in Bathurst, Bathurst New South Wales, Australia. He married (1) MARI-

Page_319.html

72. http://onlineathens.com/stories/042900/ele_list.shtml#.VeUW-JchttU

73. http://www.ebooksread.com/authors-eng/north-georgia-college/cyclops-1943-volume-37-tro/page-3-cyclops-1943-v olume-37-tro.shtml

ETTA SHINDER. He married (2) VIOLET JOYCE STUZMAN born abt 1934 in New Mexico.

Edgar Maitland Vance and Marietta Shinder had the following children:
i.   BARBARA JO VANCE born in Whittier, California. She married WITHERS.

Edgar and Violet Joyce Stuzman had two chiLdren:
ii.   RANDALL WALKER VANCE, born in Denver, Colorado.
iii. EDGAR MAITLAND VANCE, III, born in Denver, Colorado.

171. EDWARD DAVID HAIGLER, MD, (Florence Virginia[6] Vance, Henry Clay[5], Henry Clay[4], David Graham[3], William Kirkpatrick[2], Dr. Patrick[1]) was born on 7 Jul 1940. He married AMANDA TALMADGE. She was born on 8 Sep 1943. She died on 4 Feb 2016 in Alabama.

Edward David Haigler and Amanda Talmadge had the following children:
i.   EDWARD DAVID HAIGLER III was born on 7 Jul 1968. He married MARY MARGARET WAITS. She was born on 21 Aug 1968.
ii.   SUSAN TALMADGE HAIGLER was born on 7 Feb 1972 in Birmingham, Alabama, and died on 14 Feb 1972 in Birmingham, Alabama.
iii. RICHARD HAMILTON HAIGLER was born on 21 Nov 1973 in Alabama.
iv.   SUSAN TALMADGE HAIGLER was born in Alabama.

172. KATHLEEN GORDON HAIGLER (Florence Virginia[6] Vance, Henry Clay[5], Henry Clay[4], David Graham[3], William Kirkpatrick[2], Dr. Patrick[1]) was born on 3 Jul 1945 in Alabama. She married (1) WATKINS. She married (2) CHARLES BRYANT MORGAN. He was born on 11 Oct 1941 in Birmingham, Alabama. He died on 1 Dec 1998 in Alabama.

Charles Bryant Morgan and Kathleen Gordon Haigler had the following children:
i.   ELLEN CHAPPLE MORGAN was born on 30 Jul 1974. She married JOHN PAUL MUSSELMAN, Jr.
ii.   VIRGINIA VANCE MORGAN was born on 06 May 1977.

173. ALLEN BRUNDIDGE HEADLEY (Barbara[6] Allen, Cora Alline[5] Vance, Edgar Walter[4], David Graham[3], William Kirkpatrick[2], Dr. Patrick[1]) was born on 23 Mar 1929 in Rochester, New York. He died on 26 May 2008 in Pensacola, Florida. He married ANNE WIGGINS.

Allen Brundidge Headley and Anne Wiggins had the following children:
i.   BARBARA HEADLEY.
ii.   ELLEN HEADLEY.

174. BONA I ALLEN (Bonaparte[6] Allen, Cora Alline[5] Vance, Edgar Walter[4], David Graham[3], William Kirkpatrick[2], Dr. Patrick[1]) was born on 5 Sep 1936 in Georgia. He married JANE KING.

Bona I Allen and Jane King had the following child:
i.   BONA KING ALLEN was born about 1960 in Georgia.

175. LAURA LEE EDWARDS (Amelia L[6] Vance, Robert Graham[5], Edgar Walter[4], David Graham[3], William Kirkpatrick[2], Dr. Patrick[1]) was born on 16 Sep 1952. She married JACK EDWARDS.

Jack Edwards and Laura Lee Edwards had the following children:
i.   RACHEL LEE EDWARDS was born on 16 Jul 1982. She married

BRYAN MARK CONNELL who was born 21 Aug 1982 in Dallas, Texas. They have a son JACKSON MARK CONNELL born 25 Dec 2016.

ii.   HANNAH LEE EDWARDS was born on 1 Apr 1989 in Dallas, Texas. She married JOE MOORE in 2015.

176. JOSEPH EDWARD JACKSON, Jr, (Amelia L⁶ Vance, Robert Graham⁵, Edgar Walter⁴, David Graham³, William Kirkpatrick², Dr. Patrick¹) was born on 2 Mar 1955 in Decatur, Georgia. He married TERI SUE GALLAND.

Joseph Edward Jackson and Teri Sue Galland had the following children:

i.   ELIZABETH GALLAND JACKSON was born on 8 Sep 1987 in Tennessee.

ii.   JOSEPH EDWARD "TREY" JACKSON III was born on 7 Jun 1990 in Tennessee.

iii.   ALEXANDER KIRBY JACKSON was born on 26 Feb 1998.

177. CHARLES VANCE JACKSON (Amelia L⁶ Vance, Robert Graham⁵, Edgar Walter⁴, David Graham³, William Kirkpatrick², Dr. Patrick¹) was born on 1 Sep 1957 in Decatur, Georgia. He married SYLVIA BROWN. She was born on 1 Oct.

Charles Vance Jackson and Sylvia Brown raised the following child:

i.   JESSICA N BELL was born on 10 Apr 1978 in Georgia. She married BENJAMIN FOERST.

178. REBECCA NEIL HENDERSON (Bobbie Maynard⁶ Vance, Robert Graham⁵, Edgar Walter⁴, David Graham³, William Kirkpatrick², Dr. Patrick¹) was born on 26 Feb 1957 in Savannah, Georgia, . She married RICHARD GNANN. Richard Gnann and Rebecca Neil Henderson had the following children:

i.   MATTHEW GNANN was born on 8 May 1992 in Savannah, Georgia.

ii.   JAMES GNANN III was born on 10 Feb in Savannah, Chatham, Georgia.

179. ROBERT THOMAS HENDERSON (Bobbie Maynard⁶ Vance, Robert Graham⁵, Edgar Walter⁴, David Graham³, William Kirkpatrick², Dr. Patrick¹) was born on 3 Dec 1961 in Savannah, Georgia. He married HOLLY LONG.

Robert Thomas Henderson and Holly Long had the following children:

i.   HAYLEY VICTORIA HENDERSON was born on 28 Sep 1987 in Savannah, Georgia.

ii.   BRADLEY HUNTER HENDERSON was born on 4 Apr 1999 in Savannah, Georgia.

iii.   JOHN TODD HENDERSON was born on 25 Sep 2001 in Savannah, Georgia.

iv.   HANNAH LEE HENDERSON was born on 30 Jun 2004 in Savannah, Georgia.

180. LILLIAN GRACE HENDERSON (Mary Ellen⁶ Patton, Samuel N⁵, Keziah Robertson⁴ Vance, William Nicholas³, William Kirkpatrick², Dr. Patrick¹) was born on 18 Sep 1907 in Scott, Virginia, and died 8 Jun 2001 in Kingsport, Tennessee. She married JOHN HAMPTON WILLIAMS. He was born on 10 Aug 1903 in Virginia and died 12 Feb 1986. She enlisted

in the army on 19 Apr 1945.

John Hampton Williams and Lillian Grace Henderson had the following children:
  i. JOHN W WILLIAMS was born about 1925 in Virginia.
  ii. DONNY WILLIAMS was born about 1928 in Virginia.

181. LORETTA MATILDA HENDERSON (Mary Ellen[6] Patton, Samuel N[5], Keziah Robertson[4] Vance, William Nicholas[3], William Kirkpatrick[2], Dr. Patrick[1]) was born on 4 Oct 1912 in Scott, Virginia. She married LIONEL WILLIAMS.

LORETTA MATILDA HENDERSON and LIONEL WILLIAMS had the following child:
  i. MARIANNE WILLIAMS who was born 15 May 1930 in Gate City, Virginia, and died 3 Jan 2010 in La Salle, Illinois. She married IVAL E VERBAL, born 14 Mar 1925 in Dante, Virginia, and died 14 Mar 1925 in La Salle, Illinois.

182. MARY ALICE HENDERSON (Mary Ellen[6] Patton, Samuel N[5], Keziah Robertson[4] Vance, William Nicholas[3], William Kirkpatrick[2], Dr. Patrick[1]) was born on 15 Apr 1917 in Gate City, Virginia. She died on 15 Mar 2012 in Oregon. She married DELOS EUGENE RICHARDSON in 1942. He was born on 6 Nov 1911 in Illinois. He died on 18 Apr 1995 in Multomah, Oregon.

Delos Eugene Richardson and Mary Alice Henderson had the following children:
  i. DOUGLAS RICHARDSON.
  ii. DAVID RICHARDSON.
  iii. BARRY RICHARDSON.
  iv. MARY DEE RICHARDSON.

183. MABEL PATTON (Sidney Edward[6] Patton, Samuel N[5] Patton, Keziah Robertson[4] Vance, William Nicholas[3], William Kirkpatrick[2], Dr. Patrick[1]) was born on 25 Sep 1915 in Kingsport, Tennessee. She died on 11 Jan 2011 in California. She married RALPH WILLIAM BROOME on 17 Mar 1934. He was born on 11 Jul 1911 in Blacksburg, South Carolina. He died on 1 Oct 1993 in Kingsport, Tennessee.

Ralph William Broome and Mabel Patton had the following child:
  i. RALPH WILLIAM BROOME was born on 31 May 1939 in Tennessee. He died 21 Jun 1982 in Tennessee. He married (1) NANCY S NORMAN on 4 Jul 1976 in Los Angeles, California. She was born about 1949. He married (2) BRENDA CAROLYN WELLS on 20 Dec 1963 in Weber, Virginia. She was born about 1946.

184. MARY EVELYN SMALLWOOD (Ethel Grace[6] Patton, Samuel N[5] Patton, Keziah Robertson[4] Vance, William Nicholas[3], William Kirkpatrick[2], Dr. Patrick[1]) was born on 6 Mar 1903 in Granville, Indiana, and died on 24 Jan 1987 in Yorktown, Indiana. She married JOHN LEWIS MATHEW. He was born on 4 Oct 1902 in Fetterman, West Virginia. He died on 29 Jul 1956 in Muncie, Indiana.

John Lewis Mathew and Mary Evelyn Smallwood had the following children:
  i. MARGARET LUCILLE MATHEW was born 14 May 1923 in Indiana and died 18 Mar 2017. She married FOREST QUIRE on 23 Aug 1946. He was born on 18 Jan 1921 in Muncie, Indiana, and died 28

Aug 2006 in Yorktown, Indiana.
ii. LELAND GUY MATHEW was born on 31 Mar 1927 in Indiana. He married Mary Eunice Walker on 9 May 1947 in Albany, Indiana. She was born 22 Sep 1925 in Selma, Indiana.
iii. CUBA JEAN MATHEW was born about 1934 in Indiana.
iv. ROBERT LAVON MATHEW was born about 1937 in Indiana. He married Betty Jean Nigh on 16 Apr 1983 in Muncie, Indiana. She was born about 1943 in Indiana.

185. GEORGIA CATHERINE SMALLWOOD (Ethel Grace[6] Patton, Samuel N[5] Patton, Keziah Robertson[4] Vance, William Nicholas[3], William Kirkpatrick[2], Dr. Patrick[1]) was born on 28 Jan 1908 in Muncie, Indiana. She died in Mar 1995 in Albany, Indiana, . She married WILLIAM SYLVESTER CLEVENGER. He was born on 23 Aug 1905 in Matthews, Indiana. He died on 3 Nov 1991 in Albany, Indiana.

William Sylvester Clevenger and Georgia Catherine Smallwood had the following children:
i. MARVIN L CLEVENGER was born on 8 Nov 1930 in Delaware County, Indiana. He died on 5 Aug 2010 in Muncie, Indiana, .
ii. HAROLD CLEVENGER was born on 4 Jul 1932 in Indiana. He died on 26 Aug 1997 in Anderson, Indiana.

186. VIOLET SMALLWOOD (Ethel Grace[6] Patton, Samuel N[5] Patton, Keziah Robertson[4] Vance, William Nicholas[3], William Kirkpatrick[2], Dr. Patrick[1]) was born on 28 Jan 1910 in Union, Indiana. She died on 28 Jan 1987 in Yorktown, Indiana. She married HARLEN ALBERT THOMAS. He was born on 24 Dec 1901 in Harrison, Indiana, and died on 13 Jul 1957 in Muncie, Indiana.

Harlen Albert Thomas and Violet Smallwood had the following child:
i. JAMES LEROY THOMAS was born on 21 Nov 1926 in Harrison, Indiana. He died on 9 Aug 1979 in Gaston, Indiana. He married REGINA LONG.

187. DELMA SMALLWOOD (Ethel Grace[6] Patton, Samuel N[5] Patton, Keziah Robertson[4] Vance, William Nicholas[3], William Kirkpatrick[2], Dr. Patrick[1]) was born on 19 Mar 1912 in Delaware County, Indiana. She died on 2 Oct 1993 in Peru, Indiana. She married CARY GLENDELL REED. He was born on 7 Aug 1909 in Indiana and died on 14 Aug 1980 in Yorktown, Indiana.

Cary Glendell Reed and Delma Smallwood had the following children:
i. BARBARA JOANN REED was born on 24 Jan 1932 in Gaston, Indiana.
ii. JOHN SAMUEL REED was born on 19 Jan 1935 in Alexandria, Indiana. He died on 3 Feb 1995.

188. SAMUEL FREDOUS SMALLWOOD (Ethel Grace[6] Patton, Samuel N[5] Patton, Keziah Robertson[4] Vance, William Nicholas[3], William Kirkpatrick[2], Dr. Patrick[1]) was born on 24 Nov 1914 in Eaton, Indiana. He died on 20 Oct 1990 in Fort Wayne, Indiana. He married RUBY MARIE WARD. She was born on 15 Dec 1915 in Indiana. She died on 20 Jul 1983 in Muncie, Indiana.

Samuel Fredous Smallwood and Ruby Marie Ward had the following child:
i. JACKIE LEE SMALLWOOD was born on 5 Jun 1934 in Muncie, Indiana. He died on 16 Feb 1988 in Red Key, Indiana. He married LILLIAN SUE GARSER on 18 Nov 1966 in Muncie, Indiana. She

was born about 1948 in Kentucky.

189. KELSEY MINILIE SCHULTZ (Charles Patton[6] Shultz, Mary Frances[5] Patton, Keziah Robertson[4] Vance, William Nicholas[3], William Kirkpatrick[2], Dr. Patrick[1]) was born on 3 Jan 1906 in Choudrant, Louisiana. She died on 31 Oct 1985 in Houston, Texas. She married VAIDEN COSBY MARTIN. He was born on 31 Mar 1895 in Water Valley, Mississippi. He died on 8 Aug 1985 in Houston, Texas.

Vaiden Cosby Martin and Kelsey Minilie Schultz had the following children:
  i.   CHARLES HENRY MARTIN was born on 31 Aug 1931 in Houston, Texas, and died on 7 Jul 1992 in Austin, Texas. He married SYDNEY HELEN DECKER. She was born on 24 Aug 1932 in Norfolk, Virginia. She died on 6 Mar 2003 in Houston, Texas.
  ii.   JOHN MARION MARTIN was born on 29 Aug 1936 in Houston, Texas. He died on 18 Dec 1999 in Houston, Texas.

190. YVONNE SCHULTZ (Fred[6] Shultz, Mary Frances[5] Patton, Keziah Robertson[4] Vance, William Nicholas[3], William Kirkpatrick[2], Dr. Patrick[1]) was born about 1921 in Texas. She married JOHN C RANDOLPH. He was born about 1920 in Louisiana. Both children appear to have been adopted by her second husband, PHILIP JAKE BRADBURY married Dec 1950. He was born 29 Jul 1925 and died Jun 1982 in New Orleans. It appears he adopted both children.

John Carlisle Randolph and Yvonne Schultz had the following children:
  i.   JEANNIE CLAIRE RANDOLPH was born 29 Oct 1939 in New Orleans and died 29 June 1999 in Colorado. She married THEODORE EDWARD DALEY in Nov 1958. He was born 3 Dec 1933 in Galveston, Texas, and died 13 Jan 1994 in Harris, Texas.
  ii.   JOHN CARLISLE RANDOLPH BRADBURY was born 10 Oct 1941 and died 20 Apr 1961 in New Orleans.

191. FRANK ROBERT CLIFTON (Alberta[6] Kelly, Alberta Bertie[5] Patton, Keziah Robertson[4] Vance, William Nicholas[3], William Kirkpatrick[2], Dr. Patrick[1]) was born on 24 Oct 1920 in Kentucky and died on 14 Feb 2000 in Louisville, Kentucky. He married DONNAFAE GISH.

Frank Robert Clifton and Donnafae Gish had the following children:
  i.   SUSAN ELLEN CLIFTON was born on 8 Jan 1952 in Louisville, Kentucky. She died on 9 Jan 1952 in Jefferson, Kentucky.
  ii.   ROBERT CLIFTON.

192. ETHEL "DOLL" CLIFTON (Alberta[6] Kelly, Alberta Bertie[5] Patton, Keziah Robertson[4] Vance, William Nicholas[3], William Kirkpatrick[2], Dr. Patrick[1]) was born about 1925 in Kentucky. She died on 24 Dec 1965 in Jefferson, Kentucky. She married (1) IKE ENSEY. She married (2) GILBERT C SHOPE.

Gilbert C Shope and Ethel "Doll" Clifton had the following children:
  i.   KENNETH SHOPE.
  ii.   GILBERT SHOPE.

193. DORIS V CLIFTON (Alberta[6] Kelly, Alberta Bertie[5] Patton, Keziah Robertson[4] Vance, William Nicholas[3], William Kirkpatrick[2], Dr. Patrick[1]) was born on 14 Jan 1926 in Louisvillle, Kentucky. She married (1) JAMES D RENEAU. She married (2) WEBSTER BIRTLES.

Doris V Clifton had the following children:
  i.   PAMELA.

    ii.   ROBERT.

194. MARTHA BELLE WEAVER (Willie Vance[6] Kelly, Alberta Bertie[5] Patton, Keziah Robertson[4] Vance, William Nicholas[3], William Kirkpatrick[2], Dr. Patrick[1]) was born on 29 Dec 1926 in Kentucky. She died on 30 Jul 1970 in Jefferson, Kentucky. She married THEODORE (TED) DEZARN. He was born on 15 May 1922 and died on 24 Sep 1975 in Jefferson, Kentucky.

Theodore (Ted) Dezarn and Martha Belle Weaver had the following children:
    i.   CHERI DEZARN was born in Nov 1947. She married an unknown spouse on 30 Aug 1975 in Jefferson, Kentucky.
    ii.   GARY DEZARN was born on 22 Jul 1949. He married an unknown spouse on 30 Nov 1977 in Jefferson, Kentucky.
    iii.   CINDY DEZARN was born in Jan 1956.

195. CHARLES WILLIAM BRIGHT Col (Mollie[6] Patton, Charles Vance[5] Patton, Keziah Robertson[4] Vance, William Nicholas[3], William Kirkpatrick[2], Dr. Patrick[1]) was born on 6 May 1921 in Greenville, Genneessee. He died on 9 May 1985 in Columbia, South Carolina. He married MARY.

Charles William Bright and Mary had the following children:
    i.   MARY BRIGHT.
    ii.   BOBBI BRIGHT.
    iii.   MARTHA BRIGHT.

196. BENJAMIN EARL BAUMGARNER (Mary Logan[6] Cloud, Nannie Rose[5] Patton, Keziah Robertson[4] Vance, William Nicholas[3], William Kirkpatrick[2], Dr. Patrick[1]) was born on 9 Sep 1941 in Kingsport, Tennessee. He married JOAN CAMPBELL.

Benjamin Earl Baumgarner and Joan Campbell had the following children:
    i.   STUART ALLEN BAUMGARNER was born on 30 Jan 1967 in Alaska.
    ii.   ELIZABETH ANN BAUMGARNER was born on 4 May 1970 in Kingsport, Tennessee.

197. JENNY LYNN CHANEY (Jane[6] Cloud, Nannie Rose[5] Patton, Keziah Robertson[4] Vance, William Nicholas[3], William Kirkpatrick[2], Dr. Patrick[1]) was born on 14 Apr 1943. She married PHILIP ANSON RIX. He was born on 26 Oct 1942 in Toronto, Canada.

Philip Anson Rix and Jenny Lynn Chaney had the following children:
    i.   MARIA TERESA RIX was born on 23 Jul 1965. She died on 26 Nov 1980 in Richmond, Virginia.
    ii.   KATHLEEN MARIE RIX was born on 30 May 1968 in Henrico County, Virginia.

198. CAROL ROSE CHANEY (Jane[6] Cloud, Nannie Rose[5] Patton, Keziah Robertson[4] Vance, William Nicholas[3], William Kirkpatrick[2], Dr. Patrick[1]) was born on 11 Sep 1948 in Kingsport, Tennessee. She died on 21 Dec 2011 in Kingsport, Tennessee. She married JERRY HOARD. She married (2) ROGER GAIL FRYE.

Jerry Hoard and Carol Rose Chaney had the following child:
    i.   JASON AARON HOARD was born on 12 Feb 1971.

Roger Gail Frye and Carol Rose Chaney had the following child:
    ii.   TAMMY LYNN HOARD (?) was born on 17 Feb 1964.

199. WILLIAM THOMAS MEADE (Minnie Ruth[6] Patton, Victor[5] Patton, Keziah Robertson[4] Vance, William Nicholas[3], William Kirkpatrick[2], Dr. Patrick[1]) was born on 21 Feb 1947. He married STARR STEFFNER.

William Thomas Meade and Starr Steffner had the following children:
  i.   JOHN THOMAS MEADE was born on 2 Feb 1972.
  ii. JUDITH MICHELLE MEADE was born on 29 Mar 1974.

200. MICHAEL EDWARD MANNING (Francis DeSales[6] Manning, Mary Netherland[5] Vance, Samuel Netherland[4], William Nicholas[3], William Kirkpatrick[2], Dr. Patrick[1]). He married (1) SANDRA ANN. He married (2) KATHY.

Michael Edward Manning and Kathy had the following children:
  i.   COREY MANNING.
  ii. RYAN MANNING.

201. GRACE HERNDON (Earnest Franklin[6], Oliver Perry[5], James Vance[4], Keziah P[3], William Kirkpatrick[2], Dr. Patrick[1]) was born on 4 Aug 1912 in Dallas, Texas, and died on 7 Mar 1993 in Kemp, Texas. She married JAMES PATRICK "JP" JOHNSON. He was born on 17 Feb 1910 in Texas. He died in May 1983 in Kemp, Texas.

James Patrick "JP" Johnson and Grace Herndon had the following children:
  i.   LELA GRACE JOHNSON was born 18 July 1933 in Dallas, Texas, and died 4 Dec 2012 in San Antonio, Texas. She married RICHARD LEE SMITHEY who was born 5 May 1932 in Lindsay, Texas and died 8 Jan 2011 in Kerrville, Texas. They had at least one son, MARK DAVID SMITHEY, b. 3 Feb 1957 in Dallas, Texas, d. 3 Oct 1992 in Mesquite, Texas.
  ii. NINA JOYCE JOHNSON was born on 14 Sep 1935 in Dallas, Texas.
  iii. SAMUEL ERNEST JOHNSON was born 22 Jul 1938 in Dallas, Texas. He married Geraldine HARNELY on 22 Jun 1973.

202. WILLIE MINALEE HERNDON (Earnest Franklin[6], Oliver Perry[5], James Vance[4], Keziah P[3], William Kirkpatrick[2], Dr. Patrick[1]) was born on 5 Sep 1918 in Dallas County, Texas. She died on 12 Mar 2000 in Dallas, Texas. She married BERT FRANCIS ELSEY on 12 Mar 1938 in Bryan, Oklahoma. He was born on 19 Sep 1902 in Missouri. He died on 6 Dec 1994 in Dallas, Texas.

Willie Minalee Herndon and Bert Francis Elsey had the following child:
  i.   BERT FRANCIS ELSEY, Jr. was born on 25 Jun 1938 in Dallas, Texas. He married (1) LINDA JANE TRAWEEK on 30 Dec 1960 but divorced 26 Oct 1976. She was born 7 Nov 1938 and died 20 Jul 1996. He married (2) DOROTHY E WILLBANKS on 1 Dec 1977 in Dallas, Texas. She was born about 1946.

203. FAY HERNDON (Earnest Franklin[6], Oliver Perry[5], James Vance[4], Keziah P[3], William Kirkpatrick[2], Dr. Patrick[1]) was born on 26 May 1921 in Dallas, Texas. She died on 31 Jan 2008 in Madisonville, Tennessee. She married (1) CARL ROBERT ELSEY. He was born in 1909 in Dallas Texas, and died on 23 Jul 1960 in Dallas, Texas. She married (2) TOM LAROCCA who predeceased her.

Carl Robert Elsey and Faye Herndon had the following children:
  i.   LOYCE JANNETTE ELSEY was born on 26 May 1938 in Dallas, Texas. She married JOE K COKER on 26 Aug 1957 in Los Angeles,

California. He was born about 1938.

204. BILLIE GEAN HERNDON (Earnest Franklin[6], Oliver Perry[5], James Vance[4], Keziah P[3], William Kirkpatrick[2], Dr. Patrick[1]) was born on 7 Feb 1931 in Dallas, Texas. He died on 1 Nov 2013 in Durant,Oklahoma. He married ALICE FAY SHIPP who was born 31 Oct 1935 in Dallas, Texas.

Billie Gean Herndon and Alice Fay Shipp had the following child:
   i.   ROBERT JOE HERNDON was born on 7 Oct 1958 in Dallas, Texas. He died on 27 Mar 2011 in Dallas, Texas.

205. MARY KATHERINE VANCE was born 21 Apr 1937 in Bristol, Tennessee. She married WILLIAM "BILL" ROY ENGLISH on 18 Jan 1958.

Mary Katherine and Bill English had the following children:
   i.   ELIZABETH ANN "BETH" ENGLISH was born 1 April 1960 in Spokane, Washington. She married a SMITH.
   ii. SUSAN GAIL ENGLISH was born 13 September 1963 in Bristol, Tennessee. She married an OLIVER.

206. GENE DOUGLAS "GENIE" VANCE was born on 7 May 1940 in Bristol, Tennessee. She married GLEN WILLIAM "BILL" KILDAY born about 1941 on 30 Jun 1962.

Gene Douglas and Bill Kilday had the following children:
   i.   MARGARET KATHERINE KILDAY.
   ii. GLEN DOUGLAS KILDAY.
   iii. WILLIAM DOUGLAS KILDAY.

Appendix

Sources

Acts Passed at the First Session of the Twenty-fifth General Assembly of the State of Tennessee, 1843-44
https://books.google.com/books?id=R01AAQAAMAAJ
(1813 act creating the Bank of East Tennessee, Wm K listed for Greeneville branch, p 66)

Balbirnie, William, an Account Historical and Genealogical, from the Earliest Days till the Present Time of the Family of Vance in Ireland, Vans in Scotland, Anciently Vaux in Scotland and England of DeVaux in France (Latin De Vallibus.), (Cork, Ireland: JM Noblett, 1860).
https://archive.org/details/accounthistorica00balb

Barton, Benjamin Smith, M.D., The Philadelphia Medical and Physical Journal (Philadelphia, 1805)
https://books.google.com/books?id=GCgdAQAAMAAJ

The Chester Inn Historic Site, http://www.tn.gov/environment/article/the-state-owned-chester-inn. Link has been removed. Now https://www.tn.gov/environment/about-tdec/tennessee-historical-commission/redirect---tennessee-historical-commission/redirect---state-programs-for-the-tennessee-historical-commission/state-historic-sites/redirect---state-historic-sites/the-chester-inn-state-historic-site.html but not necessarily the same information.

Confederate Papers Relating to Citizens or Business Firms, 1861-65
NARA M346. Known as the "Citizens File," these original records pertain to goods furnished or services rendered to the Confederate government by private individuals or business firms
https://www.fold3.com/title/60/confederate-citizens-file#overview

East Tennessee Historical Society - Publications, volume 27 (Knoxville, Tn; 1955) (Theodotia Vance and the Sign of the Bell Inn)

Findagrave.com, a wealth of information, links are to the lists of Vances
Deck Cemetery, Washington County, VA: https://www.findagrave.com/cgi-bin/fg.cgi?page=gsr&GSiman=1&GScid=2601056&GSfn=&GSln=Vance
Old Harmony Graveyard, Greeneville, TN: https://www.findagrave.com/cgi-bin/fg.cgi?page=gsr&GSln=Vance&GSiman=1&GScid=2224876&
Oakhill Memorial Park, Kingsport, TN: https://www.findagrave.com/cgi-bin/fg.cgi?page=gsr&GSiman=1&GScid=16496&GSfn=&GSln=Vance
Glenwood Cemetery, Bristol, TN: https://www.findagrave.com/cgi-bin/fg.cgi?page=gsr&GSiman=1&GScid=12436&GSfn=&GSln=Vance
East Hill, Bristol, TN : https://www.findagrave.com/cgi-bin/fg.cgi?page=gsr&GSln=Vance&GSiman=1&GScid=50098&

Hillcrest Cemetery, Buford, GA: https://www.findagrave.com/cgi-bin/fg.cgi?page=gsr&GSln=Vance&GSiman=1&GScid=34526&

Fink, Paul M, Jonesborough: The First Century of Tennessee's First Town (Overmountain Press, 1972)

Goodspeed's History of Greene County, found online at http://www.tngenweb.org/goodspeed/greene/

Goodspeed's History of Washington County, found online at http://www.newrivernotes.com/topical_books_1887_history_of_tennessee.htm

Goodspeed Publishing, History of Tennessee, Illustrated : from the earliest time to the present, together with an historical and a biographical sketch of from twenty-five to thirty counties of east Tennessee, besides a valuable fund of notes, original observations, reminiscences, etc., etc., containing historical and biographical sketches of thirty east Tennessee counties : Anderson, Blount, Bradley, Campbell, Carter, Claiborne, Cocke, Grainger, Greene, Hamblen, Hamilton, Hancock, Hawkins, James, Jefferson, Johnson, Knox, Loudon, McMinn, Meigs, Monroe, Morgan, Polk, Rhea, Roane, Sevier, Sullivan, Unicoi, Union, Washington (1887)

Groce, W. Todd, Mountain Rebels: East Tennessee Rebels and the Civil War, 1860-1870 (Knoxville: University of Tennessee Press, 1999).

Lexington Church Records, http://files.usgwarchives.net/va/rockbridge/churches/lexpres.txt

Lyle, Oscar K, Lyle Family, The Ancestry and Posterity of Matthew, John, Daniel and Samuel Lyle, Pioneer Settlers in America (Brooklyn, NY: Lecouver Press, 1912) 292-293.

McClung, James W, The Historical Significance of Rockbridge County (Staunton, Va: McClure Company, Inc, 1939) 218-219.

Miller, Alan N., East Tennessee's Forgotten Children (Baltimore: Clearfield Co., 2001) (Indentures)

Miller, G. Howard, The Revolutionary College: American Presbyterian Higher Education, 1707-1837 (New York: New York University Press, 1976).

Morton, Oren F., A History of Rockbridge County Virginia (Staunton, Va, The McClure Company, Inc, 1920)

Owens, Joshua, A Case Study of the Founding Years of Liberty Hall Academy: The Struggle Between Enlightenment and Protestant Values on the Virginia Frontier, Journal of Backcountry Studies, vol 3 number 2 http://libjournal.uncg.edu/jbc/article/view/18

Speer, William S., Sketches of Prominent Tennesseans (Nashville, 1888 / 2003) (Charles R Vance, lawyer)

Spoden, Muriel M. C., Ancestry and Descendants of Richard Netherland, Esquire (1764-1832) (self-published, 1979)
(Descendants of Sarah Anne Netherland and Dr. William Nicholas Vance, p. 121 – 130. Incorrect reference to the Mexican American war and the sheriff of Sullivan County)

Taylor, Oliver, Historic Sullivan, a History of Sullivan County, Tennessee, with brief Biographies of the Makers of History (Bristol, TN: The King Printing Company, 1909)
(References the Draper Manuscript Collection with the story of Dr. Patrick's scalping treatment)

Vance Family Association Newsletters, membership is extremely inexpensive. http://vancefamilyassociation.org/

Vans, Jamie, P A Vans, Origin of the Irish Vances, a review of the evidence (Vans Family Archive, 1983, 2001, 2007)

Washington & Lee Library Holdings, Lexington, Virginia, original papers from family and church collections.

Ancestors of Dr. Patrick Vance

1. Dr. Patrick Vance, son of Hugh Vance, was born in 1755 in Ireland. He died in 1791 in Rockbridge County, Virginia, USA. He married Mary Graham. She was born before 1750 in Scotland. She died before 1796 in Rockbridge County, Virginia.
2. Hugh Vance, son of Thomas Vance, was born about 1743 in Gortward, County of Donegal, Ireland. He died about 1771 in Gortward, County of Donegal, Ireland.
3. Thomas Vance, son of George Vance, was born about 1710. He died in 1741 in Gortward, County of Donegal, Ireland.
4. George Vance, son of Patrick Vaus, was born about 1680 in Raneel, Ireland. He died on 7 Mar 1712 in CY, , Donegal, Ireland.
5. Patrick Vaus, was born in 1650 in Ireland. He died in Ireland.
6. Rev John Vaus, son of Sir John Vaus (Vans) and Margaret McDowell, was born in 1617 in Kikmacreenan, Ireland. He died in 1671 in Ireland.
7. Sir John Vaus (Vans), son of Sir Patrick Vaus (Vans) and Lady Catherine Kennedy, was born in 1580 in Barnbarroch, Coagh, Ireland. He died in Jun 1642 in Barnbarroch, Coagh, Ireland. He married Margaret McDowell in 1595 in Wig-

town, Wigtownshire, Scotland, daughter of Uchtred MacDowall and Margaret Stewart, was born in 1597 in Gartland, Ireland. She died in 1710 in Ireland.

8. Sir Patrick Vaus (Vans), son of Sir JOHN VANS of Barnbarroch and Janet McCulloch, was born in 1529 in Barnbarroch, Wigtownshire, , Scotland. He died on 22 Dec 1597 in Barnbarroch, Wigtownshire, , Scotland. He married Lady Catherine Kennedy in 1558 in Cassilis, Ayrshire, Scotland, daughter of Gilbert Kennedy and Dame Margaret Sophia Kennedy, was born in 1550 in Lybrack, Ireland. She died on 14 Mar 1593 in Terregles, Kirkcudbrightshire, Scotland.

9. Sir JOHN VANS of Barnbarroch, son of Sir Patrick Vans and Lady Margaret Kennedy, was born in 1510 in Barnbarroch, Scotland. He died on 10 Sep 1547 in Trabzon, Trabzon, Turkey. He married Janet McCulloch in 1526 in Myrtoun, Wigtownshire, Scotland. Janet McCulloch was born in 1507 in Myrtown, Wigtownshire, Scotland. She died in 1561 in Barnbarroch, Scotland.

10. Sir Patrick Vans, son of Alexander Vans, was born in 1469 in Wigtown, Wigtownshire, Scotland. He died in 1528 in Barnbarrock, Scotland. He married Lady Margaret Kennedy in 1498 in Wigtown, Wigtownshire, Scotland, was born in 1458 in Wigtown, Wigtownshire, Scotland. She died in 1510 in Penninghame, Wigtownshire, Scotland.

11. Alexander Vans, son of Patrick Vans and Lady Mary Kennedy, was born in 1480 in Barnbarroch, Wigtownshire, , Scotland. He died on 13 Jul 1569 in Barnbarrock, Wigtownshire, , Scotland.

12. Patrick Vans, son of Blaize Vans and Elizabeth Shaw, was born in 1459 in of Barnbarroch, , Wighton, Scotland. He died in 1528 in Barnbarroch, Wigtownshire, , Scotland. He married Lady Mary Kennedy in 1498 in Wigtown, Wigtownshire, Scotland, the daughter of Lord John Kennedy and Elizabeth Montgomerie, was born in 1460 in Wigtown, Wigtownshire, Scotland. She died in 1510 in Barnbarroch, Wigtoun, Wigtonshire, Scotland.

13. Blaize Vans, son of Robert Vans 1, was born in 1424 in Barnbarroch, Wigtonshire, Scotland. He died on 26 Feb 1481 in Barnbarroch, Wigtonshire, Scotland. He married Elizabeth Shaw in 1468 in Barnbarrock, Wigtownshire, Scotland, born in 1444 in Haillie, Ayrshire, Scotland. She died in Barnbarroch, Wigtonshire, Scotland. His father, Robert Vans 1, was born in 1384 in Barnbarrock, Wigtownshire, Scotland. He died on 30 Sep 1498 in Barnbarrock, Wigtownshire, Scotland.

14. Lord John Kennedy, son of 1st of Dunure Lord Gilbert Kennedy and Lady Catherine Maxwell, was born on 12 Oct 1436 in Maybole, Ayrshire, , Scotland. He died on 24 Jul 1508 in Maybole, Ayrshire, , Scotland. He married Elizabeth Montgomerie who was was born in 1445 in Huntly, Aberdeenshire, Scotland. She died on 17 Apr 1500 in Cupar, Fife, , Scotland Barnbarroch, Wigtownshire, Scotland.

15. 1st of Dunure Lord Gilbert Kennedy, son of James the Younger of Dunure Kennedy Sir and Mary Princess of Scotland Countess of Angus Stewart Princess, was born in 1396 in Maybole, Ayrshire, Scotland. He died on 6 Mar 1478 in Maybole, Ayrshire, Scotland. He married Lady Catherine Maxwell in 1440 in Maybole, Ayrshire, Scotland, born in 1408 in Linlithgow, West Lothian, Scotland. She died in 1484 in 1684081, Ayrshire, Scotland.

16. James the Younger of Dunure Kennedy Sir was born about 1390 in Dunure Castle, Dunure, Maybole, Ayrshire, Scotland. He died before 8 Nov 1408

in Dunure Castle, Dunure, Maybole, Ayrshire, Scotland. He married Mary Princess of Scotland Countess of Angus Stewart Princess in 1405 in Maybole, Ayrshire, Scotland. Mary Princess of Scotland Countess of Angus Stewart Princess, daughter of King Robert of Scotland Stewart III and Annabella Consort Scotland Drummond, was born in 1376 in Rothesay Castle, Isle of Bute, Scotland. She died on 20 Mar 1458 in Thrieve Castle, Galloway, Scotland.

17. King Robert of Scotland Stewart III was born in 1337 in Dundonald, Ayrshire, Scotland. He died on 04 Apr 1406 in Dundonald, Ayrshire, Scotland. He married Annabella Consort Scotland Drummond on 13 Mar 1366. She was born in 1346 in Stobhall, Scotland. She died in 1401 in Perth, Perthshire, Scotland.

Index of Family Names

Included here are only the direct family members, their spouses and their children. There are other names in the book such as spouses' parents and names in obituaries but are not included in this section. Names in parentheses are mostly maiden names but one is the adopted name of a male.

If this book undergoes any revisions, this index will not be updated. If you can't find the name on the designated page look to the next page as most likely.

www.ingramcontent.com/pod-product-compliance
Lightning Source LLC
Chambersburg PA
CBHW031532260326
41914CB00026B/1664